the
Embroidered
HOME

beautiful embroidered crafts for your home

ELLEN MOORE JOHNSON

ROCKPORT PUBLISHERS

First published in the United States of America by Rockport Publishers, Inc.
33 Commercial Street
Gloucester, Massachusetts 01930-5089
Telephone: (978) 282-9590
Facsimile: (978) 283-2742
www.rockpub.com

We have made every effort to ensure that the instructions, illustrations, and diagrams are accurate and complete. We cannot, however, be responsible for human error, typographical mistakes, or variations in individual work.

ISBN 1-56496-795-6

10 9 8 7 6 5 4 3 2 1

Design and Layout: Leslie Haimes
Cover Design: Jeannet Leendertse
Cover Images: Main image: Picture Press: Schöner Wohnen/photographer: Nüttgens; three bottom images: Bobbie Bush Photography
Photography: Bobbie Bush Photography
Illustrations: Pages 15-21, Judy Love. All other illustrations and diagrams by Lorraine Dey Studio.

Printed in China.

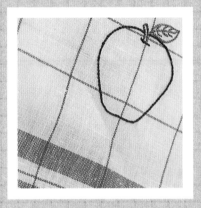

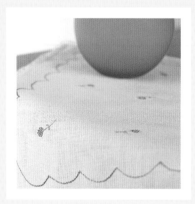

Introduction

It seems we've always been searching for new ways to bring style to our living quarters. Our fascination with transforming an ordinary dwelling into a unique personal oasis can be traced all the way back to the ancient Egyptians, the first civilization known to have embellished handwoven linen fabrics with embroidery. The desire for beautiful surroundings remains deeply embedded in our consciousness today. It is our goal to help you in your quest to create a comfortable and cozy place to live, to help you turn your dwelling into a true home.

Have you ever thought about the factors that govern the manner in which you decorate your home? Your family, your age, your career, your friends, even your hobbies—all of these things, and more—influence the decisions you make about your home's furnishings and overall decor. Many different styles result from the merging of our diverse backgrounds, but one simple common thread continues to tie us all together: We all love to create, to make things with our hands.

Perhaps you're yearning to decorate a box with beautiful stitchery. Maybe memories of cooking and chatting with Mom in the kitchen have sparked a desire to embroider a tablecloth. Whether you embroider a gift of elegant linen bed sheets to help a young couple set up house-keeping or you whip up a whimsical shower curtain for your daughter's first apartment, you are adding beauty and inspiration to the lives of those you love. The needlework you create today will be passed down to future generations and become cherished possessions that tie togeth-er a family's history. Cherished treasures that bring happiness. Heirlooms.

We invite you to join us as we embark upon our tour of The Embroidered Home. It doesn't matter whether you're a novice needleworker, a veteran stitcher, or someone who tried her hand at embroidery once upon a time but who hasn't picked up a needle in many years. Let's take a peek …

SECTION ONE: *Embroidery Basics*

Before you can begin embroidering, you must become acquainted with materials and equipment appropriate to your project. The array of fabrics, fibers, and tools available to today's needle artist is vast. Knowing which ones to choose will make your embroidery go smoother and ensure the longevity of your finished piece.

This section covers the obvious embroidery requirements—needle, stitching fiber, and background fabric—as well as auxiliary supplies, from scissors and stilettos to tracing vellum and marking chalk. You'll learn how to prepare a pattern for embroidery, transfer the design to the background fabric, and secure the fabric in a hoop or frame. Refer to this section as needed when working on an individual project. We've also diagrammed a few of the basic embroidery stitches featured in the projects to help you get started.

SELECTING NEEDLES

Many types of needles are used in embroidery, and one of the embroiderer's essential skills is the ability to select the appropriate needle(s) for a project. The needle should be slightly thicker than the thread, so that it will lay open a sufficiently large passage in the fabric for the thread to pass through. Needle size is indicated by number; the lower the number, the larger the needle.

Crewel Needles

Crewel needles, commonly referred to as embroidery needles, are sized #1 through #10. They are of medium length with a long, oval eye and a short point. Here are some recommended uses:

#7 or #8	beginning shadow work; beginning Point de Paris
#9	shadow work; Point de Paris (pinstitch); stem stitch; detached chain stitch; granitos; backstitch; cutwork
#10	shadow work (this small needle size is perfect for rendering the tiny, even stitches necessary for smooth curves); hemstitch; satin stitch; granitos; stem stitch; drawn thread work

Crewel needles #1 through #8 will accommodate three to six strands of stranded cotton, silk, rayon, coton à broder (twisted, nondivisible thread), broder medicis (fine wool thread), #8 perle cotton, #12 perle cotton, and fine metallics; crewel needles #9 and #10 will accommodate one or two strands of cotton, silk, or rayon.

Sharps

Sharps are general-purpose needles, sized #1 through #12. They are of medium length with a small, round eye and a sharp point. Here are some recommended uses:

#10	beginning bullions; hems; general sewing (e.g., fine hand sewing)
#11	small, tight bullions
#12	small, tight bullions; satin-stitched dots; tiny whip stitches for hand appliqué (superior for achieving fine detail)

Sharps #7 through #9 will accommodate two or three strands of stranded cotton, silk, or rayon; #10 through #12 will accommodate one or two strands of stranded cotton, silk, or rayon.

Milliner's Needles

Milliner's needles, also known as "straw" needles, are sized #1 through #15. They are extra long with a round eye and a sharp point. The eye is no wider than the shaft, allowing for easy manipulation of bullion wraps. Here are some recommended uses:

#8	beginning long bullions
#10	long bullions

Milliner's needles #1 through #4 will accommodate four to six strands of stranded cotton, silk, rayon, coton à broder (twisted, nondivisible thread), #8 perle cotton, #12 perle cotton, and metallics. Milliner's needles #9 through #11 will accommodate one or two strands of stranded cotton, silk, or rayon.

Tapestry Needles

The distinguishing feature of the tapestry needle is its blunt, rounded tip. This special feature enables the needle to slip easily between the warp and weft threads without piercing or snagging the fabric. Tapestry needles are sized #13 through #28. They are of medium length and have a long, oval eye. Here are some recommended uses:

#26—Fil Tiré (punch work); silk ribbon embroidery (on delicate fabrics such as handkerchief linen and swiss batiste); pulled and drawn thread embroidery; cross-stitch; petit point

#28—Fil Tiré (punch work); shadow work (the small needle size is perfect for rendering tiny, even stitches)

Tapestry needles #26 and #28 will accommodate multiple strands of stranded cotton, silk, rayon, fine metallics, and broder medicis (fine wool thread) or single strands of silk ribbon, coton à broder (twisted, nondivisible thread), #8 perle cotton, and #12 perle cotton.

Chenille Needles

Chenille needles are excellent for working with thicker threads and silk ribbon. They are sized #14 through #26. Chenille needles are of medium length with a long, wide oval eye and a sharp point. Here are some recommended uses:

#22	beginning silk ribbon embroidery
#24	silk ribbon embroidery (the sharp point proves quite useful when working on a densely woven fabric by diminishing the fraying of the ribbon)

Chenille needles #22 and #24 will accommodate tapestry wool, crewel wool, six strands of stranded cotton, #3 perle cotton, #5 perle cotton, thick silk, heavy metallics, and silk ribbon.

Betweens

Betweens, also referred to as quilting needles, are sized #1 through #12. Quite short in length, betweens have a small, round eye and a sharp point. Their small size is very good for rendering short stitches quickly and accurately. Here are some recommended uses:

#7	French knots; outline stitch
#10	running stitch; backstitch, beginning quilting; appliqué

Betweens #7 and #10 will accommodate floche à broder beautifully. Also recommended are one or two strands of cotton, silk, or rayon.

SELECTING FIBERS

The wide array of fibers available in today's marketplace makes thread selection more exciting than ever, but it can also create confusion for the embroiderer. The descriptions of fibers given here will help you appreciate their different attributes and uses.

Generally, you should match the fiber content to the background fabric. Use linen, cotton, or mercerized threads on linen or cotton fabrics, silk threads on silk fabrics, and wool threads on wool fabrics. The finished pieces will wash better because the fibers are spun to the same tension and have the same pull. When stitching items that won't be laundered frequently, you can relax the rule a bit.

Threads that fade or bleed can ruin a project, so it is very important to verify colorfastness. Even though many manufacturers label their products as colorfast, it is always wise to test any questionable threads before you begin stitching.

Some threads are particularly difficult to manipulate and tend to fray easily. Metallics, rayon, and silk fall into this category. If you choose these fibers, use short lengths—about 12" (30 cm)—to make them more manageable and to help them retain their luster.

Six-Strand Cotton Embroidery Floss

Cotton floss is the most commonly used embroidery thread. Its six mercerized two-ply strands can be separated to create different thicknesses of thread in the needle. Strands of different colors can be used together for added color depth and richness. Cotton floss is available in hundreds of colors and has a silky sheen. It is appropriate for all types of embroidery.

Overdyed Floss

Overdyed floss is usually a particular shade of six-strand cotton floss that has been dyed with additional colors to create a watercolor effect. The colors flow together in a pleasingly subtle manner, making this thread particularly useful in stitching flowers, leaves, and water.

Floche à Broder

Floche à broder is a mercerized five-ply, single-strand cotton thread that is available in over seventy colors. It has a silky sheen, and the individual strands are thicker than those in six-stranded cotton floss. Floche à broder lies very smoothly against the fabric, making it a wonderful choice for satin stitch and shadow work embroidery.

Coton à Broder

Coton à broder is a twisted, nondivisible mercerized cotton thread that is available in over one hundred colors. This versatile thread has a slight sheen and is especially good for cutwork, pulled thread, whitework, and monogramming.

Perle Cotton

Perle cotton is a mercerized, twisted, nondivisible thread. It is available in hundreds of colors and four different size gauges: #3 (the heaviest), #5, #8, and #12. Perle cotton's lustrous corded finish is good for creating textures. Recommended uses include canvaswork, needlepoint, and hardanger.

Broder Medicis

Broder medicis, also known as crewel wool, is a fine, two-ply, nondivisible yarn that can be used singly or in multiple strands. Broder medicis is the most commonly used wool thread for surface embroidery. It is available in more than one hundred colors and is quite suitable for needlepoint, crewel, and general embroidery.

Linen

Linen is a very strong, nondivisible thread. Its textured finish lends a natural effect. Primarily used to stitch on linen fabric, linen thread is available in both solid and overdyed colors.

Silk Ribbon

Silk ribbon has a lustrous finish and is favored for silk ribbon embroidery. It is available in over one hundred solid and overdyed colors and comes in four widths: 2 mm, 4 mm, 7 mm, and 13 mm. The 2 mm ribbon is excellent for small projects such as jewelry and for stitching small flowers and buds. The 4 mm ribbon is the easiest to manipulate, the most commonly used, and available in the widest array of colors. The 7 mm ribbon is useful for larger or more dramatic stitches. The 13 mm ribbon—the most expensive and the most difficult to find—works up into bold, luxuriant flowers and can be used to cover large areas quickly. Since silk ribbon frays easily, short 12" (30 cm) lengths should be used.

Silk Embroidery Floss

Silk embroidery floss has multiple strands that, like cotton floss, can be separated to create different thicknesses of thread. The individual silk strands are similar in thickness to those of cotton floss. Silk embroidery floss has a very high sheen and is available in hundreds of colors. The spectacular luster of silk makes it desirable for almost any type of embroidery. Caution is advised, however, because silk snags easily and frays quickly.

Rayon Embroidery Floss

Rayon embroidery floss is a six-strand, divisible mercerized synthetic fiber. It has a very high sheen, which makes it readily interchangeable with silk floss. Rayon floss is also usually less expensive—a bonus when cost is a factor. The disadvantages of rayon floss are that it snags easily and can be difficult to manage. The embroiderer who is willing to tackle these obstacles with patience and diligence should be well pleased with the end results, because rayon floss can provide an exceptionally striking accent to any piece of stitching.

Metallic Threads

Metallic threads are available in a multitude of colors and weights. Some metallics are actually wrapped sections of metallic plastic. These brilliant fibers add sparkle to your stitching, making them a wonderful choice for holiday projects. Due to the widely varying characteristics of metallic threads, each one should be evaluated individually.

SELECTING FABRICS

Fabrics for embroidery can be divided into two categories: evenweave and plain weave. Evenweave fabrics are those which have the same number of warp and weft threads per square inch. The exact number of threads per inch is referred to as the "count." Evenweave fabrics in durable fibers are particularly suitable for table linens. "Plain weave" refers to fabrics that are not evenly woven. Examples include dress and furnishing fabrics in both smooth and textured varieties, such as satins, slub silks, velvets, and heavy wools.

There are several factors to consider when determining the suitability of a fabric for a particular project. Will the article be used daily and laundered frequently? Do you require ease of cleaning and durability along with a dainty appearance? Or, perhaps the embroidery will be purely decorative and framed under glass. When decorative pieces will not be laundered, the fabric selection can focus more upon aesthetics and less upon practicality. The needle artist can concentrate on choosing a fabric that works with the embroidery to convey a particular mood or feeling.

A final question is whether the piece is intended as a future heirloom and, as such, requires special consideration. An example of this type of article is a ringbearer's pillow—it must be fashioned from materials that are elegant yet able to withstand a child's inevitable touching and poking. Again, the question of washability arises. In all likelihood, such a piece will become soiled with handling and will require cleaning, particularly if the family plans to pass it on for use by future generations. A fabric that must fulfill so many requirements has to be selected carefully. While each situation is different, it is advisable to remember the advantages of using washable fabrics when soiling is a possibility.

Also be sure the fabric quality is worthy of the time you will spend on the embroidery. The importance of using good-quality fabrics cannot be overemphasized. Fabrics can be woven from man-made materials, natural fibers, or a combination of the two. For keepsake or heirloom pieces, natural fiber fabrics are preferable. Natural fiber textiles will endure for many generations when properly maintained. Here's a look at four fiber types you might use.

Cotton

Cotton is one of the most abundantly available fabrics today. Four kinds of cotton plants provide the raw materials for textile manufacturers. Sea Island cotton plants produce the finest-quality fibers, followed by Egyptian cotton plants, American Upland varieties and, finally, Asiatic plants. The majority of cotton fabric is manufactured from American Upland cotton varieties. Cotton yarn can be woven into many different kinds of fabrics. Batiste, broadcloth, cambric, crepe, drill, gingham, huck, lawn, nainsook, organdy, percale, piqué, poplin, sateen, swiss, and velveteen are but a few examples of cotton's versatility.

Linen

Linen yarn and cloth are produced from fibers obtained from the flax plant. Flax that has been harvested late in the summer produces the best-quality linen. The majority of the world's linen is produced in Europe. Belgium, France, and Ireland have become famous for their fine-quality linen fabrics. Cambric, damask, huck, and lawn are a few examples of linen fabrics.

Silk

Silk, one of the strongest natural fibers, is produced by silkworms. Each silkworm in its lifetime produces between 500 and 1,300 yards of fiber. The raw silk is reeled off the cocoons, twisted tightly into skeins, and shipped to manufacturers of silk fabric. Silk is very smooth and elastic. Dirt does not easily cling to it, making it one of the most useful materials of the textile world. The different ways of weaving and finishing silk provide a wide variety of finished materials: crepe, moiré, piqué, poplin, satin, shantung, and velvet, to name a few.

Wool

Wool yarn and cloth are produced from the sheared coats of sheep, goats, and members of the camel family. Most wool is obtained from Merino sheep flocks, but the African and Asian camel, alpaca, angora goat, cashmere goat, llama, and vicuna provide textile manufacturers with other special kinds of wool. Wool is primarily used for articles of clothing because it acts as a natural insulator. Shielding the body from varying outside temperatures, wool keeps a person cool in the summer as well as warm in the winter. Broadcloth, cashmere, crepe, and flannel are examples of wool cloth.

EMBROIDERY FRAMES

There are two advantages to using an embroidery frame. One advantage is that the work remains clean and unrumpled. Another is the uniformity of stitch tension. There is no better way to perfect your stitching technique than by working on a piece of fabric that is held taut and secure in a frame.

Embroidery frames are available in different shapes and sizes. The two most commonly used are ring frames, or hoops, and scroll frames. The mounting of embroidery fabric into a frame is called "dressing the frame." The most important point to remember when dressing any type of frame is that the fabric must be stretched with the warp and weft threads running at right angles to one another to prevent distortion.

Hoops can be made of wood, plastic, or metal. They are available in many sizes, the most common being 4", 5", 6", 8", and 10" (10 cm, 13 cm, 15 cm, 20 cm, and 25 cm). Round frames in larger sizes are often available with a table clamp attachment that includes screws for adjusting the angle and height of the frame. Round frames with table or floor stands are yet another option.

Small hoops are suitable for embroidery designs that can fit within the ring diameter. This way, the entire design can be stitched without having to reposition the fabric in the frame. The best type of round frame has an adjustable screw on the outer ring, allowing for even distribution of tension across the surface of the hooped fabric. Spring-type round frames do not produce this result and are not advised. There's a lot of tension on the fabric when it is in the hoop. To avoid damaging delicate fabrics, wrap the inner ring with cotton tape before dressing the frame.

Scroll frames, usually made of wood, are extremely versatile. They have two rollers, each with a cloth strip attached, to which the edge of the embroidery fabric is stitched. The rollers are held apart and parallel by side bars. Pegs in the side boards can be moved to adjust the frame to the appropriate size. The rollers may be turned to move the fabric or regulate the tension. Scroll frames can accommodate small or large pieces of work. They may be purchased with table or floor stands, or used alone as a lap frame.

THE EMBROIDERER'S WORKBASKET

While every needle artist's workbasket is unique, there are some items no embroiderer should be without.

- Embroidery scissors (for cutting threads)
- Dressmaker's shears (for cutting fabric)
- Paper scissors
- Tape measure
- Ruler
- Silk pins and pincushion
- Fine-line water-soluble pen (to mark embroidery design lines on fabric)
- Soft lead (#2) pencil (to mark embroidery design lines on fabric)

- Tailor's chalk (to mark sewing lines on fabric)
- Tracing paper (lightweight and heavy vellum)
- Graph paper
- Pounce powder and pad
- Tracing wheel
- Dressmaker's carbon
- An assortment of needles
- Thimble(s)
- Fingershield
- Stiletto
- Needlecase
- Thread organizer
- Assorted small hoops
- Cloth tape (to wrap the inside ring of round frames)

Scissors

The temptation to use the most conveniently located pair of scissors can be great, especially when only a few threads need snipping. Resist the urge to engage in scissor swapping. Scissors that are used to cut paper become dull very quickly, and dull scissors will damage intricate stitching. The blades will "chew" the fabric and threads instead of neatly cutting and trimming them.

Two pairs of sharp scissors are needed for embroidery—a pair of 6" (15 cm) or 8" (20 cm) dressmaker's shears for cutting fabric and a small pair of embroidery scissors, usually about 3" (8 cm) in length, for trimming threads and cutting intricate shapes or holes. Embroidery scissors should have very sharp, narrow, pointed blades with perfectly closing tips. All sewing and needlework scissors must be kept sharpened, and each pair should be stored in its own sheath when not in use. Scissors purchased without a protective sheath should be stored in a scissor case.

Other types of scissors that may prove helpful in various situations are lace scissors and blunt pocket scissors. Lace scissors are small scissors with a 1/4" (5 mm) duckbill at the ends. The special duckbill feature allows you to trim away excess fabric without accidentally snipping the lace. Blunt pocket scissors are used for general trimming. They are small with rounded tips, but the blades are very sharp.

Good scissors are costly, but the investment is worthwhile. Stitching is much more enjoyable when done with appropriate and properly maintained equipment.

Pins

Only premium-quality silk pins are acceptable when working with fine fabrics. Poor-quality pins have dull points and rough shafts. These defects can mar beautiful cloth and ruin hours of work. Many poor-quality pins have plastic heads that will melt onto the material when touched with a hot iron. Premium-quality pins have very sharp points, smooth shafts, and metal or glass ball heads. These pins glide through the fabric and do not melt if pressed over with a hot iron. Always avoid sewing over pins with a sewing machine to eliminate the possibility of breaking the needle or damaging the machine.

Thimbles and Fingershields

Thimbles and fingershields, used properly, can prevent the misery of sore fingers so often endured by avid stitchers. Thimbles are caps or guards used to protect the middle finger of the stitching hand when pushing a needle through fabric. In a properly fitted thimble, the pad of the finger should almost touch the bottom. On the outside, thimbles must be deeply pitted to catch the eye of the needle; a smooth finish prevents roughening of the thread. An embroiderer working on a fixed frame will require two thimbles—one for the hand beneath the frame and the other for the hand that works on top.

Fingershields are plastic or leather forms that fit over the index finger of the nonstitching hand. Fingershields prevent nicks and scratches caused by the sewing motion of a needle.

Stilettos and Awls

Stilettos and awls are pointed instruments that are used for forming holes in fabric without cutting or breaking the fibers. The point is used to spread the fibers apart. A stiletto is wide at the base, or handle end, and tapers gradually to a point. An awl is the same diameter from the base to the beginning of the pointed tip. While both tools are used in stitching eyelets, stilettos are more common.

PROPER LIGHTING

Eye fatigue is a common problem for needle artists. A very bright light and a magnifying glass will help alleviate the symptoms associated with overstrain. Fluorescent lamps are preferable because they emit "cool" light. Nonprescription reading glasses or a magnifying glass that can be hung around the neck are both viable magnification options. A wonderful invention and worthwhile investment is the magnifier lamp. This fully adjustable swing-arm lamp features a magnifying glass encircled by a fluorescent bulb.

Many optometrists recommend a stitching regimen that consists of thirty-minute work sessions interspersed with ten-minute breaks. This practice, coupled with the use of appropriate lighting and magnification devices, should eliminate virtually all eye fatigue.

TRANSFERRING THE DESIGN TO FABRIC

There are three popular methods for transferring embroidery designs to fabric: direct tracing, dressmaker's carbon, and pricking and pouncing. With each method, accuracy is extremely important. Sloppily transferred designs can result in imprecisely placed stitches that distort the original pattern. There is nothing more disheartening than spending hours of stitching time only to be disappointed with the final product because the design appears lopsided or does not align properly on the straight grain of the fabric. Readying your project for stitching can seem like a dull chore, particularly when you can barely wait to thread your needle, but doing it properly is essential.

Preparing the Fabric

First, preshrink the fabric by laundering it according to the manufacturer's guidelines. You can skip the preshrinking step only if the finished piece will not be washed. Apply spray starch over the entire surface of all fabrics except silk until slightly damp. After the cloth has absorbed the starch, iron it until dry. For silk fabrics, simply press with a warm iron. If you are embroidering on a cut piece of fabric, zigzag the outer edges on a sewing machine, or overcast them by hand, to prevent fraying. This step is obviously not necessary when embroidering a purchased article, such as a kitchen towel or pillowcase.

Before actually transferring an embroidery design to fabric, you must determine its placement. The most common practice is to center the design on the fabric. To find the center of the fabric quickly, fold it in quarters and mark the intersection of the two crease lines with a water-soluble pen or by inserting a straight pin. Use the same folding method to locate the center of your paper template, and mark it with a colored pen.

Direct Tracing Transfer

The direct tracing transfer method is easy to do. It is most successful with light-colored and delicate fabrics.

1. Trace or photocopy the embroidery design onto heavy vellum to create a template. If needed, outline the design with a black felt-tip pen so that it will be darker and easier to see when the fabric is placed over it.

2. Tape the design template to a smooth, flat, light-colored surface, such as a countertop, a solid-surface cutting board, or a piece of sturdy white corrugated cardboard. Place the fabric to be embroidered on top of the template (you should be able to see the design through the fabric). Make sure the design is properly centered and/or aligned, and then tape down the fabric.

3. Using a soft lead (#2) pencil or a fine-line water-soluble pen, trace the design onto the fabric. Work slowly and carefully; an accurately transferred design always results in a more beautifully stitched piece. If the design lines are difficult to read through the fabric, try taping the template and fabric to a light box or a large sunny window for tracing instead.

Dressmaker's Carbon Transfer

The dressmaker's carbon transfer method requires the use of a special fabric carbon and a stylus. Fabric carbons are available in several different colors, so select one that will stand out when it is applied to the material. This method is suitable for densely woven and dark-colored fabrics.

1. Trace or photocopy the embroidery design onto heavy vellum to create a template.

2. Tape the fabric to a clean, flat surface, such as a countertop. Place the design template on top of the fabric, making sure it is centered and/or aligned.

Secure the template to the fabric by taping around three edges only. Leave the fourth edge open.

3. Slip a piece of carbon paper, colored side down, through the opening so that it is sandwiched between the fabric and the design template. Tape down the fourth edge of the template.

4. Go over the design lines with a stylus or ballpoint pen, making sure to capture all the fine details. Work slowly and carefully; an accurately transferred design always results in a more beautifully stitched piece.

5. Lift one corner of the template and carbon paper to assure that the design has transferred successfully. Retrace any faint lines before removing the papers.

Pricking and Pouncing

Pricking and pouncing is the traditional method of transferring a design for embroidery. Appropriate for any type of fabric, this method is particularly effective on textured cloth, such as damask, shantung, and velveteen.

1. Trace or photocopy the embroidery design onto heavy vellum to create a template.

2. To make a pricker, insert the eye end of a #24 chenille needle into a cork.

3. Place the design template right side down on a piece of felt. Use the pricker to pierce holes along all design lines, spacing them about $1/16$" (less than 2 mm) apart. Hold the pricker in an upright position to ensure clean perforations. Work slowly and carefully; an accurately transferred design always results in a more beautifully stitched piece.

4. Tape the fabric to a clean, flat work surface, or pin it to a padded ironing board. Place the perforated design template smooth side down on top of the fabric. Make sure the template is centered and/or properly aligned, and then secure it to the fabric with tape or pins.

5. Pour a small amount of pounce powder or grated colored chalk into a dish. Dip a cotton ball into the powder, and shake off any excess. Dab the powder onto the perforations. When the entire design has been covered, carefully remove the template.

6. To see the transferred outline more clearly, connect the dots using a water-soluble pen or tailor's chalk.

Removing Transfer Marks

The transfer marks produced by direct transfer, dressmaker's carbon, and pounce powder or grated chalk should be easily removable by hand washing, particularly if the fabric was pretreated with spray starch. Use a mild detergent in cool water, and rinse well. To mark nonwashable fabrics, use pounce powder only and gently dust off the remaining residue with a soft brush when you are through.

Always test the chosen transfer method on a scrap of the project fabric and make sure the marks are removable before transferring the entire design. To run a test, cut a small swatch of the project fabric. Apply a test pattern—for example, your name—to the swatch using the selected transfer method. Test the washability by laundering in cool water with a mild detergent. If transfer marks remain on the fabric, select another method and repeat the testing. Continue the process until a desirable outcome is achieved.

TIPS AND TECHNIQUES

Every needle artist enjoys learning new tips to enhance the stitching process. The helpful hints gathered here will aid in your mastery and enjoyment of the art of embroidery.

- Always work with short thread lengths, cut no longer than 20" (51 cm). Longer lengths are uncomfortable to manipulate and tend to fray or twist. Shorter lengths, not exceeding 12" (30 cm), are recommended for fibers that fray easily, such as silk ribbon.

- Needle eyes are machine-cut, which creates a distinct front and back to the eye hole. If you experience difficulty threading a needle, try turning the needle around and threading it from the opposite side. Needle threaders can be helpful, too.

- Cut—do not break—embroidery thread. Threads that are broken tend to fray and are difficult to thread into the eye of a needle. Make sure the end you insert into the needle eye is trimmed neatly.

- Use a waste knot for tying on. Thread the needle, and make a knot at the end of the thread. Insert the needle into the fabric from the right side approximately 6" (15 cm) to the left of the starting point. Draw through so the knot rests on top of the fabric. Bring the needle up through the fabric at the selected starting point and begin stitching. When you are finished, clip the knot. On the underside, thread the tail into the needle and weave it into the back of the work.

- To tie off, or end a thread, push the threaded needle through to the back of the fabric and weave it in and out of three or four neighboring stitches.

- To mount very delicate fabrics such as organdy or swiss batiste in a round frame, use white tissue paper in addition to wrapping the inner hoop with cotton tape. Sandwich the fabric between single sheets of tissue, mount the paper and the fabric together, and then tear away the paper from the center of the hoop where the embroidery is to be done. The paper that remains acts as a protective barrier between the fabric and the frame.

- Always remove the embroidered piece from a round frame at the end of each stitching session to prevent marking or stretching the fabric.

- If a design falls too close to the edge or corner of the fabric, mounting the piece in an embroidery frame can seem impossible. The solution is to extend the fabric with a false edge. First, tear or cut a square of muslin that will extend at least 4" (10 cm) beyond the circumference of the frame. Next, center the edge or corner to be embroidered on top of the muslin. Baste the two layers of fabric together. Finally, carefully cut away the muslin behind the area to be embroidered. Mount the piece in the frame and stitch the design. Remove the basting stitches and muslin when the embroidery is completed.

- Before embroidering a design that has been transferred by pricking and pouncing, spray the chalk marks with hairspray. Hairspray acts as a fixative to inhibit smudging and fading. A caveat: Never use hairspray on silk fabric, and spot-test all fabrics before attempting this method.

- Always wash your hands and dry them thoroughly before each stitching session. Even if your hands appear clean, your natural skin oils and residues from hand lotions and cosmetics can cause soiling.

STITCH LIBRARY

Stem Stitch

STEP 1: Bring the thread to the front of the fabric on the left end of the design line (point A). Hold down the thread with your left thumb, and insert the needle into the fabric on the design line slightly to the right (point B). Bring the tip of the needle out midway between points A and B (point C).

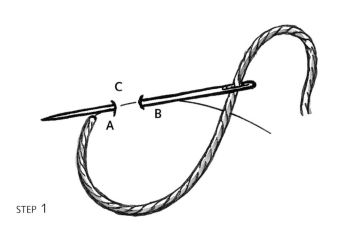

STEP 1

Continue holding down the thread with your thumb as you pull the thread through to set the first stitch.

STEP 2: Insert the needle into the fabric on the design line slightly to the right of point B. Bring the needle to the front again at point B (in exactly the same hole). Hold the thread down with your left thumb and pull the thread through to set the second stitch. Continue working the embroidery in this way. Try to make all of the stitches about 1/8" (3 mm) in length.

To tie off, take the needle to the back at the end of the

design line. Anchor the thread with three or four small loop knots.

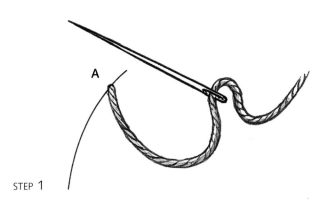

STEP 1

Backstitch

STEP 1: Bring the thread to the front of the fabric a short distance from the right end of the design line (point A).

STEP 2: Insert the needle into the fabric at the end of the design line (point B). Bring the tip of the needle out on the design line to the left of point A (point C). Pull the thread through to set the first stitch.

STEP 3: Reinsert the needle into the fabric at point A (in exactly the same hole). Bring the tip of the needle out on the design line to the left of point C (point D). Pull the thread through to set the second stitch. Continue working the embroidery in this way. Try to make all the stitches about 1/16" (less than 2 mm) in length.

STEP 2

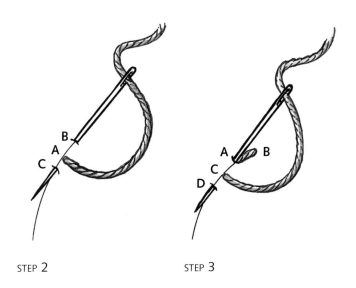

STEP 2   STEP 3

Interlaced Backstitch

Interlaced backstitch is actually a combination stitch. First, work the backstitch along the design line, and tie off.

Thread a #28 tapestry needle with the same or a contrasting thread. Bring the needle to the front of the fabric under the first stitch at the right end of the backstitched design line (between points A and B). Weave the needle in and out, alternately, under the backstitches. Take care not to pierce either the fabric or the backstitch threads.

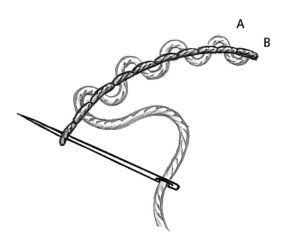

Straight Stitch

Bring the needle to the front of the fabric (point A). Insert the needle back into the fabric (point B) for the desired stitch length, and then bring it out at the beginning of the next stitch (point C). Straight stitches can be worked uniformly or irregularly, depending upon the effect you wish to achieve. It is best to keep them short in length and resting firmly against the ground fabric; they tend to snag when they are too long or too loose.

To tie off, take the needle to the back on the last stitch. Anchor the thread with three or four small loop knots.

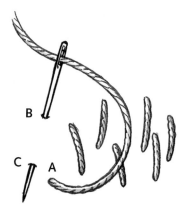

To tie off, take the needle to the back on the last stitch at the end of the design line. Anchor the thread with three or four small loop knots.

Double Backstitch (a.k.a. Shadow Work)

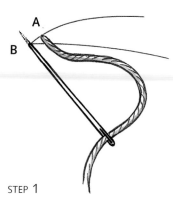

STEP 1

STEP 1: Bring the thread to the front of the fabric on the upper design line, a short distance from the tip of the shape (point

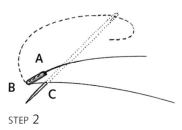

STEP 2

A). Insert the needle back into the fabric at the tip (point B). Pull through to complete the first stitch.

STEP   2:

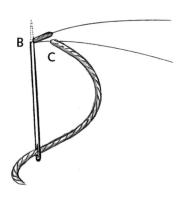

STEP 3

Reemerge on the lower line of the shape a short distance from the tip (point C).

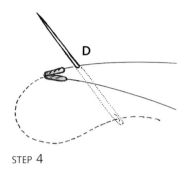

STEP 4

STEP 3: Reinsert the needle into the fabric at point B (in exactly the same hole). Pull the thread through to complete the second stitch.

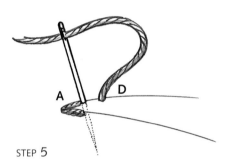

STEP 5

STEP 4: Bring the needle and thread to the front of the fabric

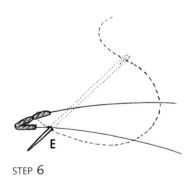

STEP 6

a short distance from point A (point D).

STEP 5: Reinsert the needle into the fabric at point A (in exactly the same

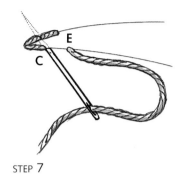

STEP 7

hole). Pull the thread through to complete the third stitch.

STEP 6: Reemerge on the lower line of the shape (point E).

STEP 7: Take the needle to the back at point C (in exactly the same hole). Pull the thread through to complete the fourth stitch.

STEP 8: Continue working the double backstitch in this man-

STEP 8

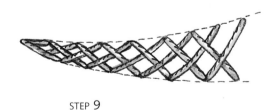

STEP 9

ner until you reach the end of the design lines. Try to make all the stitches about 1/16" (less than 2 mm) in length. In designs where one line is shorter, such as curved shapes, work the stitches on the shorter inside line slightly smaller so that each pair of backstitches moves in tandem.

STEP 9: On the reverse side, the threads should cross over one another. The crisscrossing threads create the "shadow" seen

Padded Satin Stitch/Satin Stitch

Follow all four steps for a padded satin stitch. For small shapes that don't require padding, omit step 2. For a plain satin stitch, omit steps 1 and 2 and simply embroider from edge to edge to fill the designated area.

STEP 1: Backstitch around the outline of the shape.

STEP 2: Fill the shape with tiny straight stitches that run perpendicular to the direction the satin stitch will be worked. This type of filling stitch is called "seeding."

STEP 3: Begin at the widest part of the shape. Use an up-and-down stabbing motion for the best results. Bring the needle to the front just outside the backstitched outline (point A). Pull the needle through, and take it to the back on the opposite side (point B), angling the needle under the outline. Continue working satin stitches very close together until half of the shape is covered.

STEP 4: Begin at the widest part again to work satin stitches over the remainder of the shape. The padded satin stitch is now complete.

To tie off, take the needle to the back and carefully weave the tail through the threads on the underside of the satin-stitched shape.

Overcast Stitch

Overcast stitch is a combination stitch that forms a smooth raised line. It is very useful for working monograms and the outlines of shapes.

First, work a row of stem stitch (page 15) along the design line. Then cover the row of stem stitch with tiny straight stitches. The straight stitches should be worked at a right angle to the padding row of stem stitches. A small amount of fabric should be picked up with each stitch that is taken, and the stitches should be made close together so that no ground fabric shows through.

To tie off, take the needle to the back and gently weave the tail through the threads on the underside of the overcast stitched line.

STEP 1

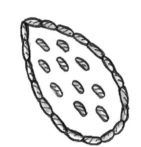

STEP 2

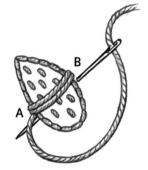

STEP 3

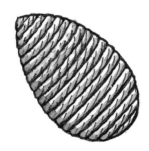

STEP 4

Detached Chain Stitch (a.k.a. Lazy Daisy)

STEP 1: Bring the needle to the front of the fabric at point A. Reinsert the needle into the fabric at point A (in exactly the same hole), and then bring the needle back up at point B.

STEP 2: Loop the thread counterclockwise so it passes under the needle. Push the needle through the fabric. Hold the thread loop lightly with your left thumb, and pull the needle gently away from you. Release the thread from your left thumb as the loop decreases in size.

STEP 3: Continue pulling the thread away from you until the loop lies flat against the surface of the fabric.

STEP 4: To anchor the stitch, take the needle to the back of the fabric just over the looped thread.

Chain Stitch

Chain stitch is actually a continuous row of detached chain stitches. Begin by working steps 1–3 for the detached chain stitch. (In other words, make a lazy daisy stitch, but don't anchor it down.)

STEP 5: Reinsert the needle into the fabric at point B (in exactly the same hole). Bring the needle back out at point C to finish the first stitch and to start the second stitch.

STEP 6: Continue working the embroidery in this way, making each stitch about 1/8" (3 mm) in length.

To tie off, insert the needle into the fabric just over the looped thread and take it to the back (Detached Chain Stitch, step 4). Anchor the thread with three or four small loop knots.

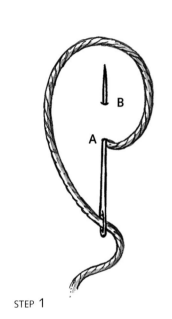

STEP 1

STEP 2

STEP 5

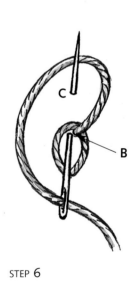

STEP 6

STEP 3

STEP 4

from the right side of the fabric.

To tie off, weave the tail of the thread through the crisscrossed stitches on the back, taking care not to pierce the fabric. Weaving back and forth three or four times will enhance the shadow effect.

Buttonhole Stitch

STEP 1: Bring the needle to the front of the fabric. Holding the thread down with your left thumb, insert the needle into the fabric at point A and come back out at point B. Still holding the thread down with your left thumb, pull the needle through the fabric and over the working thread.

STEP 2: Repeat the step 1 motion. The stitches in the illustra-

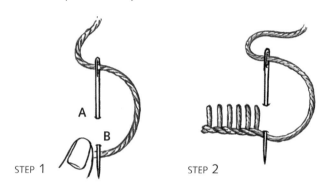

STEP 1   STEP 2

tion are slightly separated to clarify the technique, but you should work yours close together so that no ground fabric shows through.

To tie off, take the needle to the back on the last stitch at the end of the design line. Anchor the thread with three or four small loop knots.

Fly Stitch

STEP 1: Bring the thread to the front at point A. Insert the needle back into the fabric to the right at point B, and bring it through below at point C. Loop the thread counterclock-

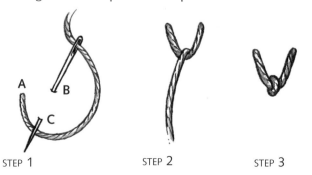

STEP 1   STEP 2   STEP 3

French Knot

STEP 1: Bring the needle to the front of the fabric at the place where the knot is to be positioned. Hold the thread taut between your left thumb and index finger approximately 1" (3 cm) away from the surface of the fabric.

STEP 2: Using your left hand, wrap the thread once around the needle.

STEP 3: Hold the thread taut again, and insert the point of the needle into the fabric one or two threads away from the starting point. Push the needle to the back of the fabric, all the while holding the thread down with your left thumb. Release your thumb as you pull the thread through to the back to set the French knot.

STEP 4: A completed French knot. If yours resembles a "Granny's bun" hairstyle, then you've done it right! For a more prominent knot, wrap the thread twice, or even three times, in step 2.

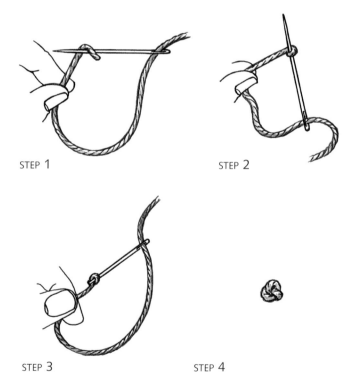

STEP 1   STEP 2

STEP 3   STEP 4

Bullion Stitch

STEP 1: Bring the needle to the front of the fabric at point A and pull the thread through. Insert the needle into the fabric at point B and bring it out again at point A, taking care not to split the thread. The thread should be to the right of the needle. Note: The distance between point A and point B should be the desired length of the finished bullion stitch.

STEP 2: From the underside, apply light pressure with the middle finger of your left hand to raise the point of the needle up off the fabric surface. Wrap the thread clockwise around the needle once, pulling tightly so the thread rests firmly against the surface of the fabric. Wrap the thread four or five more times around the shaft of the needle, keeping the wraps as even as possible.

STEP 3: Pull the thread with your right hand until the wraps are compacted together and rest firmly against the surface of the fabric. The wraps should be fairly snug, but not so tight as to bind the needle.

STEP 4: Hold the wraps in this position by placing your left thumb on top of them and your left index finger directly underneath on the underside of the fabric. Draw the needle and thread away from you, through the fabric and the wraps. The wraps should remain stationary as the thread slides through. Remove your left thumb and pull the needle and thread away from you again to ensure that the wraps are packed tightly together at the end of the thread emerging at point A.

STEP 5: Next, pull the thread firmly toward you. Use your left thumb to push the wraps snugly against the surface of the fabric.

STEP 6: The bullion stitch is now in place between points A and B. Anchor the stitch by inserting the needle into the fabric at point B and taking it to the back.

STEP 7: The finished bullion stitch looks like this. Note that the number of wraps required is determined by length of the stitch and the type of thread.

Tie off on the underside with three or four small loop knots.

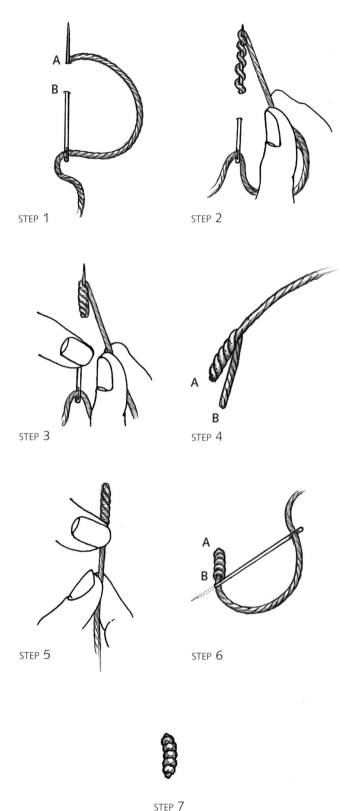

STEP 1

STEP 2

STEP 3

STEP 4

STEP 5

STEP 6

STEP 7

SECTION TWO: *Projects*

A snuggly wool throw for the living room, a charming tea cozy for the kitchen, elegantly monogrammed bed linens for the boudoir, fluffy cotton towels for the bath—these projects and twenty-six more (not to mention a host of variations) can be found on the following pages. The featured projects are organized room by room to give you lots of innovative ideas for decorating your own home. Venture with us into the embroidered living room, the embroidered kitchen and dining room, the embroidered bedroom and bath to see the delightful wonders you can create with needle and thread. A gallery section follows, brimming with accessories, small accent pieces, and gift ideas, many of which can be stitched in just a few hours.

To ensure your stitching satisfaction, each featured project has been carefully designed and tested, and then assigned a skill level:

Beginner, or Brush-up

Intermediate, or Some experience

Advanced, or Been stitching for quite a while

So that you can see at a glance what a project entails, we've also included a complete list of materials, a roster of the stitches used, a thread color guide, and a time estimate for completing the project. Photographs, clear step-by-step instructions, and full-color illustrations all work together to provide you with a foolproof strategy for successful stitching. You'll find additional stichery guidlines in the gallery section. Let's get started!

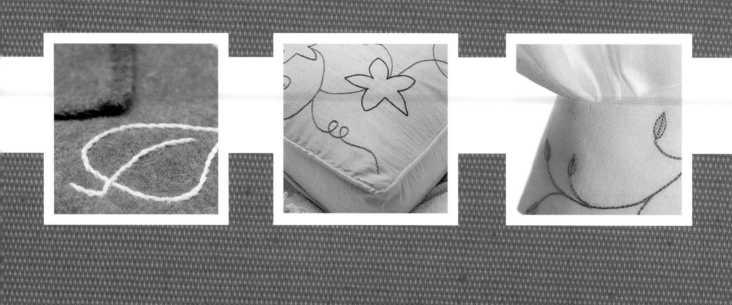

THE EMBROIDERED *Living Room*

The living room is a gathering place—a place where family members recount their daily experiences, as well as celebrate special occasions. Nothing is more inviting than a living room decorated to convey the unique personality of the family who dwells there. Whether you prefer furnishings that are boldly modern or elegantly traditional, you can personalize the main living area of your home with your own hand embroidery.

Imagine, if you will, a sleek, stark, contemporary room. The leather sofa by the fireplace looks inviting enough, but add a beautifully hand-stitched sage green blanket to the picture and you've created a homey spot that invites snuggling up with a good book. It's this kind of special attention to style and comfort that makes a house a home.

The projects in this chapter are designed to help you turn your living room into a haven for your family. Three of the projects—a silk dupioni cushion cover, linen curtain panels, and a wool throw—are stitched on ready-made pieces, making them all the more appealing because there's no finishing work involved. Simply embroider and enjoy! The fourth project—an exquisite mahogany storage box—requires only minimal finishing.

Of course, you can adapt any of the projects to fit your own décor. Changing the color palette or using a different stitch can significantly alter the appearance of a piece. Take a look at the project variations for ideas on working these designs into your overall decorating theme.

- GREEN WOOL THROW; OURS MEASURES 66" × 96" (168 CM × 244 CM)
- TWO 30-YARD (27-METER) SKEINS OF 3-PLY TWISTED SILK/MERINO WOOL YARN; WE USED SILK & IVORY 02 WHITE
- #24 CHENILLE NEEDLES
- EMBROIDERY SCISSORS
- 5" (13 CM) ROUND EMBROIDERY HOOP
- TAPE MEASURE
- SILK PINS (STRAIGHT PINS WITH GLASS OR METAL HEADS)
- PAPER SCISSORS
- TRANSPARENT TEMPLATE PLASTIC
- BLACK FINE-LINE FELT-TIP PEN
- TAILOR'S CHALK PENCIL

STITCH USED
STEM STITCH (PAGE 15)

 SKILL LEVEL
BEGINNER

 ESTIMATED TIME REQUIRED
8–10 HOURS

Wool Throw with leaves

Create a snuggly conversation piece for your living room when you embellish a ready-made throw with your hand embroidery. Single ivory-colored leaves drift downward against a ground of heathered green washable wool. The entire design is worked in stem stitch, making this a perfect project for a beginner. If the soft, natural palette isn't right for your living room's color scheme, try a bolder combination, like red and white or blue and yellow.

☐ WHITE SILK/WOOL 3-PLY YARN

Wool Throw with leaves

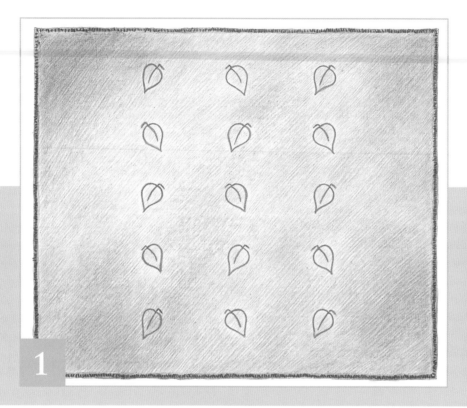

1

STEP 1 Using a black fine-line felt-tip pen, trace leaves A and B (page 112) three times each onto transparent template plastic. Cut out the six transparent templates with paper scissors. Fold the wool throw into quarters to locate the center, and mark with a straight pin. From the center, measure toward the longer edges of the throw 22" (56 cm) in each direction, and mark with pins. Pin two A and three B leaf templates—evenly spaced—along this 44" (112 cm) axis. Trace around the edge of each template with a tailor's chalk pencil. Remove the pins and templates. From the center axis, measure toward the shorter edges of the throw 20" (51 cm) in each direction, and mark with pins. Pin three A and two B leaf templates along each of these columns, even with the center axis leaves. Trace the leaf outlines. Remove all the pins and templates.

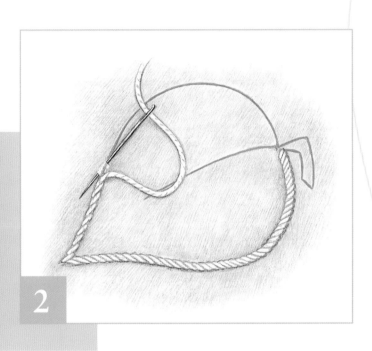

2

VARIATION

For an appealing twist, reverse the color scheme—stitch the leaves in sage green yarn on a winter white wool throw. Just for fun, make two companion throws, reversing their colors.

STEP 2 Embroider the fifteen leaves in stem stitch, using one strand of silk/wool yarn in a #24 chenille needle. Start each leaf at the base of the stem. Embroider around the perimeter, including the stem outline (or embroider a single-line stem, as shown in the project photo). End by stitching the vein down the middle of the leaf.

Use the template patterns on page 112.

- 16 × 16" (41 CM × 41 CM) SILK DUPIONI CUSHION COVER (PURCHASED OR SEWN FROM A COMMERCIAL PATTERN)

- SIX-STRAND COTTON EMBROIDERY FLOSS; WE USED ONE SKEIN EACH DMC #550, #552, #554, 3362, 3364

- #9 CREWEL NEEDLES

- EMBROIDERY SCISSORS

- 3" × 5" (8 CM × 13 CM) OVAL EMBROIDERY HOOP

- SILK PINS (STRAIGHT PINS WITH GLASS OR METAL HEADS)

- DRESSMAKER'S CARBON PAPER

- STYLUS

STITCH USED
CHAIN STITCH (PAGE 19)

SKILL LEVEL
BEGINNER

ESTIMATED TIME REQUIRED
10–12 HOURS

Silk Sofa Pillow

Dress up your sofa with this simple, elegant cushion. Regal purple flowers, sprigs of lavender berries, and lush green tendrils are joined by delicate violet swirls, all on a ground of butter-colored silk dupioni. The entire design is worked in chain stitch on a purchased cushion cover, making this project ideal for a beginning stitcher. The experienced seamstress may prefer to buy fabric yardage and custom-sew the pillow using a commercial pattern.

 PURPLE DMC #550

  VIOLET DMC #552

 LAVENDER DMC #554

 JADE DMC #3362

 MOSS DMC #3364

Silk Sofa Pillow

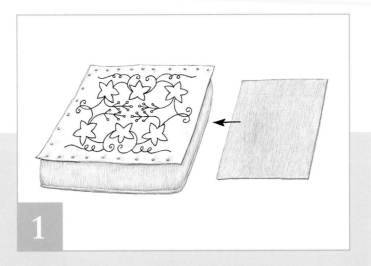

STEP 1 Unzip the cushion cover and remove the down pillow insert. Make two mirror-image copies of the template pattern (page 112). Tape both halves together, berries toward the middle, to fit the top of the cushion cover. Follow the Dressmaker's Carbon Transfer instructions (page 12) to mark the design on the front of the cushion cover.

STEP 2 Thread a #9 crewel needle with two strands of purple floss. Anchor the top layer of cushion fabric in the hoop so one of the star-shaped flowers is showing. Begin the chain stitch embroidery at the tip of one of the petals. When you reach the base of the petal, anchor the stitch to keep the inside angle sharp. Continue embroidering up the base of the adjacent petal, this time anchoring the stitch at the petal's tip. Continue embroidering all around in this manner until you reach the starting point. Tie off.

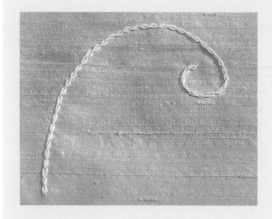

3

STEP 3   Repeat step 2 to embroider each of
the remaining star-shaped flowers. Embroider the
other design lines in chain stitch in the same way,
using violet floss for the connecting swirls, the
two greens (one strand of each) for the tendrils,
and lavender for the sprigs of berries.

Use the template pattern on page 112.

VARIATION

If your décor calls for a more neutral
color palette, if you prefer a more understated look, or if you just want to simplify the project, try stitching the entire
design in ecru-colored thread on taupe
silk dupioni. You can also change the
purple-and-green color scheme to match
your existing home furnishings. Either
way, you'll create a beautiful cushion.

DMC ECRU

- WHITE LINEN TIE-ON CURTAIN PANELS, 54" × 96" (137 CM × 244 CM) (PURCHASED OR SEWN FROM A COMMERCIAL PATTERN)
- SIX-STRAND COTTON EMBROIDERY FLOSS; WE USED TWO SKEINS EACH OF DMC #320 AND #368, ONE SKEIN EACH OF #792 AND #793
- #10 CREWEL NEEDLES
- EMBROIDERY SCISSORS
- 5" × 7" (13 CM × 18 CM) OVAL EMBROIDERY HOOP
- SILK PINS (STRAIGHT PINS WITH GLASS OR METAL HEADS)
- DRESSMAKER'S CARBON PAPER
- STYLUS

STITCHES USED
STEM STITCH (PAGE 15)
DETACHED CHAIN STITCH (A.K.A. LAZY DAISY) (PAGE 19)

SKILL LEVEL
INTERMEDIATE

ESTIMATED TIME REQUIRED
APPROXIMATELY 45 MINUTES FOR EACH PATTERN REPEAT

Linen Curtain with Vine and Simple Flowers

Vivid periwinkle flowers and graceful green vines on a ground of white linen conjure up images of a South Seas paradise. The delicate embroidery on these airy, lightweight panels is sure to add a touch of mystery and tropical romance to your home. The design requires only two stitches: stem stitch and detached chain stitch. As always, you can alter the color scheme to suit the décor of your home, no matter where you live.

 DARK LEAF GREEN DMC #320

 LEAF GREEN DMC #368

 INDIGO DMC #792

PERIWINKLE DMC #793

Linen Curtain with Vine and Simple Flowers

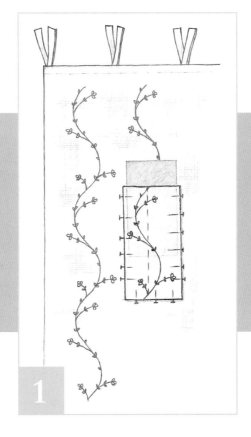

STEP 1 To mark this repeating design, begin at the upper left corner of the curtain panel. Following the instructions for Dressmaker's Carbon Transfer (page 12), mark one vine repeat (page 113) 1" (3 cm) below the top edge and centered between two pairs of tie tabs. Be sure to align the vertical dashed lines on the template with the fabric grain. Mark the second repeat directly below it so the vine continues uninterrupted. Continue in this way until the design has been transferred down the entire length of the panel; then repeat across the width.

STEP 2 For the foliage, thread a #10 crewel needle with the two green flosses (one strand of each). Starting at the top and working down, embroider the vines and stems in stem stitch. Work the leaves in detached chain stitch. Continue in this way until you have embroidered all of the foliage.

TIEBACKS

Tiebacks create subtle elegance, gracefully drawing a curtain aside to reveal an outdoor view. In this design, shadow work leaves sprout from a meandering stem stitch vine.

For each tieback, you will need two 9" × 18" (23 cm × 46 cm) pieces of white linen. Photocopy the template pattern (page 113) twice, once in mirror image, and tape the two halves together. Using the Dressmaker's Carbon Transfer method (page 12), mark the full tieback outline on one piece of linen, and mark the embroidery design on the half that will show at the window. Thread a #10 crewel needle with two strands of leaf green floss. First, embroider all of the vines in stem stitch. Next, work double backstitch to create the shadow work leaves. End by backstitching a vein down the center of each leaf.

To assemble the tieback, pin a 9" × 18" (23 cm × 46 cm) piece of medium-weight nonfusible interfacing to the back of the embroidered linen. Machine-baste along the marked outline. Place the embroidered linen and the plain linen pieces right sides together, and pin through all the layers. Machine-stitch along the basting line, leaving a 3" (8 cm) opening for turning. Trim the seam to 1/4" (5 mm) and zigzag to prevent fraying. Turn the tieback right side out, press the seams with a warm iron, and slip-stitch the opening closed. Tack small rings to each end. Your tieback is ready to use!

STEP 3 For the flowers, thread a #10 crewel needle with two strands of indigo floss. Make a small detached chain stitch in the center of each flower petal. Then, using two strands of periwinkle floss, make a larger detached chain stitch around each dark blue center.

Use the vine repeat template pattern on page 113.

 LEAF GREEN DMC #368

- MAHOGANY STORAGE BOX
- 10" × 10" (25 CM × 25 CM) SQUARE OF IVORY SILK DUPIONI
- SIX-STRAND COTTON EMBROIDERY FLOSS; WE USED TWO SKEINS OF DMC #550 AND ONE SKEIN EACH OF #869, #420, #3362, #3364
- #8 CREWEL NEEDLES
- #9 CREWEL NEEDLES
- EMBROIDERY SCISSORS
- 5" (13 CM) ROUND EMBROIDERY HOOP
- SILK PINS (STRAIGHT PINS WITH GLASS OR METAL HEADS)
- DRESSMAKER'S CARBON PAPER
- STYLUS
- IRON AND IRONING BOARD

STITCH USED

STEM STITCH (PAGE 15)

BACKSTITCH (PAGE 15)

SATIN STITCH (PAGE 18)

SKILL LEVEL

ADVANCED

ESTIMATED TIME REQUIRED

12–14 HOURS

PURPLE DMC #550

BROWN DMC #869

CHESTNUT DMC #420

JADE DMC #3362

MOSS DMC #3364

Storage Box with Grapes

Plump vineyard grapes dangle from a sturdy stem, enticing you to peek inside this handcrafted mahogany box to see what treasures you may find. The embroidery is worked on a ground of ivory silk dupioni. The look is luxurious, despite the fact that only three stitches are used to complete the design. The extensive use of satin stitch provides the ideal opportunity for perfecting your technique. After all, practice makes perfect!

Storage Box with Grapes

STEP 1 Iron the silk dupioni to remove any wrinkles. Follow the Dressmaker's Carbon Transfer instructions (page 12) to center and mark the grapes design (page 113) on the silk fabric. Thread a #9 crewel needle with one strand each of brown and chestnut floss. Secure the fabric in the embroidery hoop so that the woody vine is showing. Embroider the vine in stem stitch. Use the same brown threads to embroider the curly tendril to the right of the grapes in stem stitch.

STEP 2 For the leaves, thread a #9 crewel needle with two strands of jade floss. Work the outer portion of each leaf in satin stitch: bring the needle to the front of the fabric on the inner line, reinsert it on the outer line, and pull through. Continue stitching in this manner all around. Thread a #9 needle with one strand each of jade and moss floss. Embroider the leaf veins and the curled tendrils in stem stitch.

VARIATION

Use the grape design to create an heirloom similar to the antique tablecloth on the front cover of the book. Simply stitch the design in white thread on a white tablecloth, and voila! You'll have a keepsake that would make a welcome addition to any family's linen closet.

STEP 3 To outline the grapes, thread a #9 crewel needle with two strands of purple floss. Starting at the top of the cluster, carefully backstitch around each grape. Make the stitches $1/16"$ (less than 2 mm) in length to ensure a smooth edge for the satin stitch that will follow. To fill the grapes, thread a #8 crewel needle with three strands of purple floss. Once again, start at the top of the cluster and work downward. Bring the needle and thread out of the fabric at the lower left edge of the grape, reinsert it at the opposite edge, and pull the thread through. Note how the first stitch is angled across the widest part of the area to be filled. Fill the top half of the grape first, then the bottom half. Repeat to fill all of the grapes in the cluster.

Use template pattern on page 113.

THE EMBROIDERED Dining Room and Kitchen

What do you enjoy most about your kitchen? Is it baking chocolate chip cookies (with the help of the children) on a Saturday morning? Sitting down to a cup of coffee and the newspaper in the breakfast nook? Or is your kitchen primarily a work space where you prepare meals that are served in the dining room?

Kitchens and dining rooms are traditionally warm, inviting places where family members and friends share everything from after-school snacks to holiday dinners. Families are turning to the kitchen as their prime gathering place, and in many regions, the dining room has been incorporated into the kitchen's floor plan to create a large, casual area for entertaining. Whether your house features this newer building trend or you have a more traditional layout with a separate dining room, you can personalize the heart of your home with accessories you embroider by hand.

The four creative projects in this chapter are designed to add a big helping of charm to the culinary center of the home. Three of the projects—a tea cozy, kitchen towel, and tablecloth and napkins set—are stitched on ready-made pieces, making them all the more appealing because there's no finishing work involved. Simply embroider and begin using your new accessories! A fourth project—a charming patchwork chair cushion—requires some sewing and finishing.

You can adapt any of our projects to fit your décor simply by changing the color palette or using a different stitch. Because even small changes can significantly alter the appearance of a piece, take your time when evaluating your options. The suggested variation for each project can help you visualize the possibilities.

- WHITE LINEN TEA COZY (PURCHASED OR SEWN FROM A COMMERCIAL PATTERN)
- SIX-STRAND COTTON EMBROIDERY FLOSS; WE USED ONE SKEIN EACH OF DMC #550, #552, #727, #973, # 972, #905, #906
- #9 CREWEL NEEDLES
- EMBROIDERY SCISSORS
- 6" (15 CM) ROUND EMBROIDERY HOOP
- SILK PINS (STRAIGHT PINS WITH GLASS OR METAL HEADS)
- DRESSMAKER'S CARBON PAPER
- STYLUS

STITCH USED
STEM STITCH (PAGE 15)

SKILL LEVEL
BEGINNER

ESTIMATED TIME REQUIRED
2–3 HOURS

Pansy Tea Cozy

Add a touch of charm to your afternoon tea with this cheerful purple and yellow pansy. The entire design is worked in stem stitch on a purchased tea cozy, for a terrific beginner's project. The experienced seamstress has the option of buying white linen fabric yardage and sewing the cozy from a commercial pattern.

PURPLE DMC #550

VIOLET DMC #552

BUTTERCUP DMC #727

LEMON SUNSHINE #973

SUNFLOWER DMC #972

GRASS DMC #905

KEY LIME DMC #906

Pansy Tea Cozy

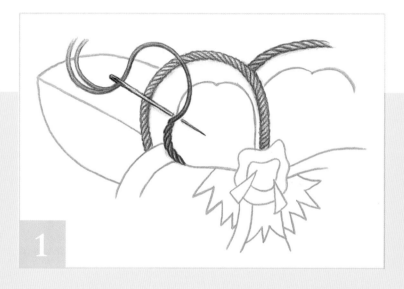

1

STEP 1   Remove the padded liner from the tea cozy. Follow the Dressmaker's Carbon Transfer instructions (page 12) to mark the pansy design on the front of the cozy. Thread a #9 crewel needle with two strands of violet floss. Embroider the outside line of each top petal in stem stitch. Change to two strands of purple floss to embroider the inner scalloped lines. For sharper definition between the scallops, pull the needle through to the back at the end of a scallop, reemerge one or two threads below and one or two threads to the left, and resume stitching. Work the three yellow petals the same way, using one strand each of buttercup and lemon sunshine floss for the outside line and two strands of buttercup for the inside line.

2

If you prefer pansies that are all one color, or if you're just looking for a way to simplify the project, try stitching the entire flower in purple. Another palette option is to let your favorite variety of pansy inspire your choice of thread colors. Either way, this cheerful addition to teatime is sure to make you smile!

STEP 2 Thread a #9 crewel needle with two strands of purple floss. Embroider the pansy's center "rings" and zigzags in stem stitch. For sharply defined zigzag points, repeat the step 1 technique: bring the needle to the back at the point, reemerge a few threads away, and resume stitching. Continue embroidering in this manner until all of the zigzag lines in the center of the pansy are stitched. Use two strands of sunflower floss to work the two triangular pistils in stem stitch. For the leaves, change to one strand each of grass and key lime floss. Outline each leaf in stem stitch.

Use the template pattern on page 114.

Tie-on chair cushion with cherries

MATERIALS

- COMMERCIAL PATTERN FOR A TIE-ON CHAIR CUSHION
- FOUR 6" × 6" (15 CM × 15 CM) SQUARES OF WHITE COTTON FABRIC
- COORDINATING FABRIC, TRIMS, ETC. (AS SPECIFIED ON PATTERN)
- SIX-STRAND COTTON EMBROIDERY FLOSS; WE USED ONE SKEIN OF DMC #321
- #9 CREWEL NEEDLES
- EMBROIDERY SCISSORS
- 4" (10 CM) ROUND EMBROIDERY HOOP
- SILK PINS (STRAIGHT PINS WITH GLASS OR METAL HEADS)
- RULER
- #2 PENCIL
- REMOVABLE TAPE
- SPRAY STARCH
- IRON AND IRONING BOARD
- DRESSMAKER'S SHEARS
- SEWING MACHINE

STITCHES USED
STEM STITCH (PAGE 15)
STRAIGHT STITCH (PAGE 16)

SKILL LEVEL
BEGINNER

ESTIMATED TIME REQUIRED
1–2 HOURS FOR EACH MOTIF

 CHERRY RED DMC #321

Let clusters of bright red cherries lend their country charm to your kitchen. This redwork project is perfect for beginners, with its easy-to-learn stitches: stem stitch and straight stitch. To make the chair cushion, start with a purchased pattern and adapt it for embroidery. You might try our checkerboard arrangement, described in the instructions, or perhaps you'll position a cluster of cherries in each corner or at the center. Some previous sewing experience is advised. If sewing isn't your forte, find an experienced seamstress with whom you can barter—you embroider something for her, and she, in return, can assemble and finish a set of cushions for you.

Tie-on Chair Cushion with Cherries

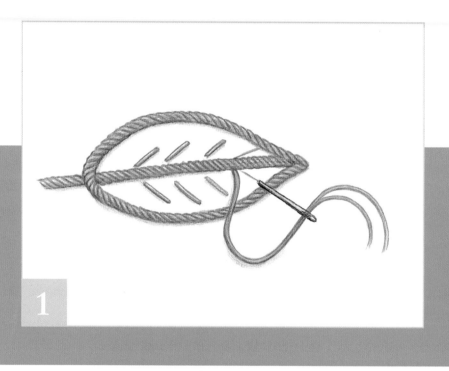

STEP 1 Follow the Direct Tracing Transfer instructions (page 12) to mark the cherry design (page 114) on each square of white fabric. Thread a #9 crewel needle with two strands of cherry red floss. Embroider each design, working the branch, stems, cherries, and, finally, leaves. Begin each leaf at the base, stitch all around, and then work the vein down the center. Embroider the tiny lateral veins in straight stitch, drawing the needle out at the center vein and reinserting it about 1/8" (3 mm) away. To avoid a thread shadow, slide the needle under the center vein stitching on the underside and bring it into position for the next lateral vein stitch.

VARIATION

The cherry design can be embroidered on dishtowels, café curtains, place mats, and napkins to create a complete kitchen ensemble. If you'd like more realistic cherries, simply add some color. Use lime peel green floss for the leaves and light brown floss for the branch and stems. Here's the complete palette:

■ CHERRY RED DMC #321

■ LIME PEEL DMC #3346

■ LIGHT BROWN DMC #434

STEP 2 Cut five 6" × 6" (15 cm × 15 cm) squares of coordinating fabric (we used a red-and-white check). Arrange the four embroidered squares and five coordinating squares in a checkerboard pattern. Pin the squares together in rows, and machine-stitch, using a $1/2$" (1 cm) seam allowance. Then join the rows together to create a 16" × 16" (41 cm × 41 cm) cushion top. Proceed with the purchased pattern and the additional supplies to complete the chair cushion.

Use the template pattern on page 114.

- LINEN DISH TOWEL
- SIX-STRAND COTTON EMBROIDERY FLOSS; WE USED ONE SKEIN EACH OF DMC #498, #321, #815, #434, #3346, #988
- #8 CREWEL NEEDLES
- #9 CREWEL NEEDLES
- EMBROIDERY SCISSORS
- 5" (13 CM) ROUND EMBROIDERY HOOP
- SILK PINS (STRAIGHT PINS WITH GLASS OR METAL HEADS)
- DRESSMAKER'S CARBON PAPER
- STYLUS
- IRON AND IRONING BOARD

STITCHES USED
CHAIN STITCH (PAGE 19)
BACKSTITCH (PAGE 15)
STEM STITCH (PAGE 15)
SATIN STITCH (PAGE 18)

SKILL LEVEL
INTERMEDIATE

ESTIMATED TIME REQUIRED
4 HOURS

Kitchen Towel with Apple Motif

Enjoy an orchard harvest year-round with this embellished kitchen towel.

Our juicy Red Delicious apple looks realistic enough to pluck off the window-pane-checked linen ground, but closer examination reveals a fruit that is not the eating kind. Four simple stitches are used: chain stitch, backstitch, stem stitch, and satin stitch. Quick and easy to embroider on a purchased linen towel, the apple will surely add a cheerful note to your kitchen. Your handwork would also make a thoughtful gift for a new bride.

DARK RED DMC #498

CHERRY RED DMC #321

CRIMSON DMC #815

LIGHT BROWN DMC #434

LIME PEEL DMC #3346

GREEN APPLE DMC #988

Kitchen Towel with Apple Motif

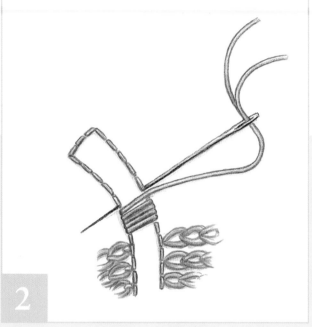

STEP 1 Fold the kitchen towel in half lengthwise and crease lightly with a warm iron. Follow the Dressmaker's Carbon Transfer instructions (page 12) to mark the apple design (page 114) on the towel; center it on the crease about 7" (18 cm) above the bottom edge. Thread a #8 crewel needle with one strand each of dark red, cherry red, and crimson floss. Beginning at the stem, work chain stitch on the apple outline all around. Continue stitching concentric rings of chain stitch until the entire shape is filled. Tie off.

STEP 2 For the stem, thread a #9 crewel needle with two strands of light brown floss. Backstitch along the apple stem outline. To fill in the stem, use satin stitch. Bring the needle and thread to the front of the fabric along one edge, insert the needle into the fabric on the opposite edge, and pull the thread through to the back to complete the first stitch. Continue to work satin stitch over the top half of the stem, then start at the middle and work in the other direction to satin-stitch the bottom half. Tie off.

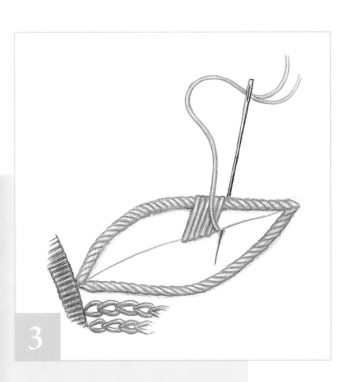

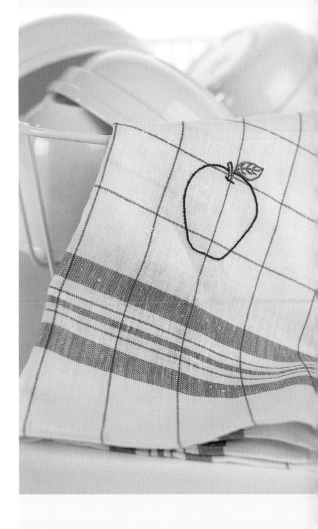

STEP 3 For the leaf, thread a #9 crewel needle with one strand each of lime peel green and green apple floss. Starting at the base, embroider the leaf outline in stem stitch. To fill in the leaf, use satin stitch. Bring the needle and thread to the front of the fabric on the vein, insert the needle back into the fabric on the leaf outline, and pull the thread through to the back to complete the first stitch. Note how the stitch lies at a slight angle. Continue working satin stitches in this manner until you reach the leaf tip, and tie off. Embroider the area on the opposite side of the vein in the same way, and then embroider the lower half of the leaf, working toward the base. Finally, embroider the leaf vein in stem stitch, using two strands of green apple floss. Tie off.

Use the template pattern on page 114.

VARIATION

For a quicker finish, work stem stitch on the design outlines only. If you prefer a different variety of apple, simply change the thread colors to suit your taste. Golden Delicious apple lovers can replace our vibrant reds with a softer yellow palette. Granny Smith aficionados could use vivid greens on a plain white towel for a striking effect.

- WHITE LINEN TABLECLOTH AND NAPKINS
- SIX-STRAND COTTON EMBROIDERY FLOSS; WE USED THREE SKEINS OF DMC #841
- #9 CREWEL NEEDLES
- EMBROIDERY SCISSORS
- 5" (13 CM) ROUND EMBROIDERY HOOP
- SILK PINS (STRAIGHT PINS WITH GLASS OR METAL HEADS)
- TAPE MEASURE
- #2 PENCIL
- REMOVABLE TAPE
- SPRAY STARCH
- IRON AND IRONING BOARD

STITCH USED
DOUBLE BACKSTITCH (A.K.A. SHADOW WORK) (PAGE 16)

SKILL LEVEL
INTERMEDIATE

ESTIMATED TIME REQUIRED
2 HOURS FOR EACH TABLECLOTH MOTIF

45 MINUTES FOR EACH NAPKIN MOTIF

Scrollwork Tablecloth and Napkins

TAUPE DMC #841

Dinner guests will feel like royalty when they sit down to a meal at your splendidly appointed table. Embroider these elegant designs for a stunning addition to your linen trousseau. In double backstitch, also known as "shadow work," the designs are worked on ready-made table linens, making this project even more desirable because there's no finishing required.

Tablecloth and Napkins

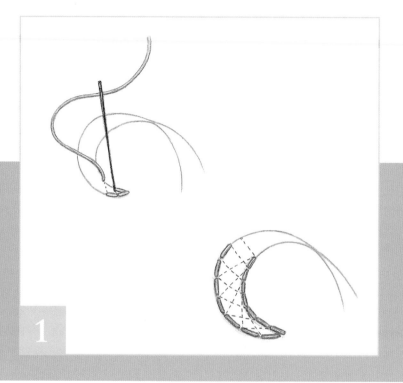

STEP 1 Apply a light coat of spray starch to the entire surface of the tablecloth. Allow two or three minutes for the fabric to absorb the starch, then iron the tablecloth dry. Follow the Direct Tracing Transfer instructions (page 12) to mark the large scroll design (page 115) on each corner of the tablecloth. Thread a #9 crewel needle with two strands taupe floss. Start in the lower left quadrant of the design. Embroider the scroll lines in double backstitch, remembering to work stitches on the inside curve smaller than those on the outside, in order to keep each pair of stitches moving along at the same pace. Continue until all four corner motifs are embroidered.

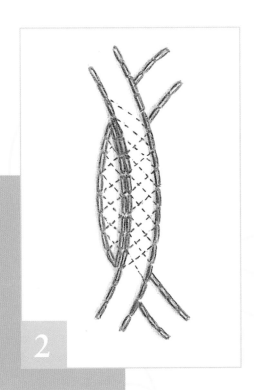

2

STEP 2 Starch and iron each napkin as you did for the tablecloth. Fold the napkin in half diagonally, finger-press lightly at one corner, and unfold. Mark the small scroll design (page 115) on the napkin corner, using the crease for alignment. Thread a #9 crewel needle with two strands of taupe floss. Embroider the scroll lines on the left half of the design in double backstitch. Tie off. Work the right half the same way. When you reach the intersection of the design lines, work one line of double backstitches directly alongside the existing stitches, so that they share the same holes. Work the remainder of the motif as usual. Tie off. Repeat for each napkin.

Use the template patterns on page 115.

VARIATION

To re-create the elegant look of antique linens, try embroidering scroll designs in padded satin stitch, shown above in progress. The embroidery will take considerably longer to complete than shadow work, but the finished linens will possess an unmistakable heirloom quality. Choose a thread color that coordinates with your fine china.

PASTEL BLUE DMC #800

THE EMBROIDERED *Bedroom*

The English translation of boudoir *is "private retreat." Certainly, with today's busier-than-ever lifestyles, there is no better place for recharging from life-on-the-run than the privacy of your own bedroom. Transform yours into a relaxing, personal sanctuary—a place where you feel as comfortable working on your needlework projects as you do drifting off to sleep on your hand-embroidered bed linens.*

Regardless of the decorative style of your bedchamber, the presence of your own hand embroidery will make it feel even more snug and intimate. Outside distractions will melt away when you cuddle up in a soft, warm, monogrammed blanket, or sink your head into a pillow embroidered with spring's most delicate blossoms. Seeing beautiful stitchery up close, every day, will rejuvenate your soul.

Three of the projects in this chapter—crisp bed linens, a cuddly Merino wool blanket, and a hemstitched cotton bedskirt—started out as ready-made pieces. It doesn't matter what size bedding you use as the designs are readily adaptable. Just choose the styles and colors that are appropriate for your furnishings and décor, and then take them one beautiful step further by adding touches of hand embroidery. The remaining project—a delicate silk lampshade—requires a little bit of finishing that you can easily do yourself. The results are both unique and exquisite.

If you're interested in trying out some different color options, or perhaps are seeking a project that requires less stitching time, be sure to consider the project variations.

- WHITE LINEN HEMSTITCHED SHEET AND PILLOWCASES
- SIX-STRAND COTTON EMBROIDERY FLOSS; WE USED TWO SKEINS OF DMC #597 AND ONE SKEIN EACH OF DMC #598 AND #3046
- #9 CREWEL NEEDLES
- #7 BETWEENS NEEDLES
- EMBROIDERY SCISSORS
- 5" × 7" (13 CM × 18 CM) OVAL EMBROIDERY HOOP
- SILK PINS (STRAIGHT PINS WITH GLASS OR METAL HEADS)
- FRAY PREVENTER MEDIUM
- RULER
- TAPE MEASURE
- #2 PENCIL
- TRACING PAPER
- BLACK FINE-LINE FELT-TIP PEN
- REMOVABLE TAPE
- SPRAY STARCH
- IRON AND IRONING BOARD

STITCHES USED
DOUBLE BACKSTITCH (PAGE 16)
FRENCH KNOT (PAGE 20)

SKILL LEVEL
INTERMEDIATE

ESTIMATED TIME REQUIRED
8 HOURS FOR TOP SHEET
4 HOURS FOR EACH PILLOWCASE

AQUAMARINE DMC #597

ICY AQUA DMC #598

WHEAT DMC #3046

Bed Linens

Dress your bed for dreaming with exquisitely hand-embroidered bed linens.

Icy aqua diamonds and bold aquamarine flowers form a simple repeat pattern

for edging a top sheet and pillowcases. Add an optional wheat-colored

monogram, pictured on page 65, using our custom alphabet. When you

start with ready-made hemstitched linens, all you do is add your handwork.

Sweet dreams!

Bed Linens

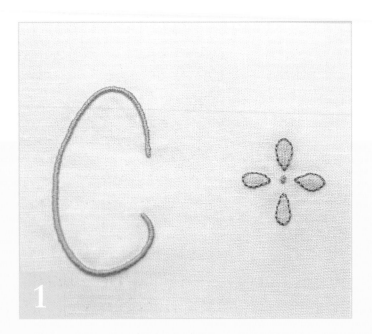

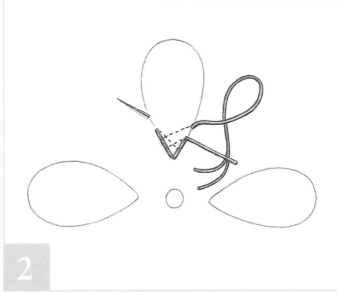

STEP 1 Apply a light coat of spray starch to the entire surface of the top sheet. Allow two or three minutes for the fabric to absorb the starch, then iron the sheet dry. Measure in 7 1/2" (19 cm) from the middle of the top edge, and mark with a pin. Follow the Direct Tracing Transfer instructions (page 12) to mark the flower-and-diamond design (page 115) across the sheet; center the middle flower at the pin. Thread a #9 crewel needle with one strand each of aquamarine and icy aqua floss. Working from left to right, embroider each diamond motif in double backstitch. Remember to work the stitches on the inside diamond smaller, in order to keep each pair of backstitches moving along at the same pace. Weave in the ends to enhance the shadow effect.

STEP 2 Thread a #9 crewel needle with two strands of aquamarine floss. Working from left to right, embroider the flowers in double backstitch. Work each petal individually, starting at the pointed end and tying off after the petal is completed. To enhance the shadow effect, repeat the step 1 technique for weaving in the ends.

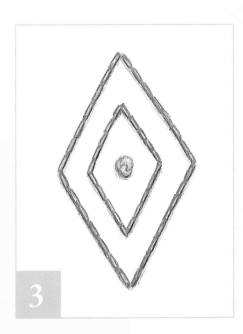

3

STEP 3 Thread a #7 betweens needle with two strands of wheat floss. Knot the thread 3" (8 cm) from the end. Working from left to right, embroider a 3-wrap French knot in the middle of each diamond and each flower motif. After drawing the thread to the back, clip it 3" (8 cm) from the end. Tie the two 3" (8 cm) tails together in a square knot, trim 1/4" (5 mm) from the knot, and seal the knot with a a dot of fray preventer.

Repeat steps 1–3 to mark and embroider each pillowcase.

Use the template pattern on page 115.

VARIATION

Make your bed linens even more sumptuous with an elegant embroidered monogram. To make the embroidery template, omit the center flower and trace one of the letters from our monogram alphabet (page 125) in that spot instead; you may wish to open up the spacing around the letter a little bit. Once you've made your template, transfer the design to your bed linens. Embroider the monogram in overcast stitch (page 18), using two strands of wheat floss.

- IVORY MERINO WOOL BLANKET; OURS MEASURES 66" × 96" (168 CM × 244 CM)
- BRODER MEDICIS WOOL THREAD; WE USED THREE SKEINS OF DMC #8685
- #24 CHENILLE NEEDLES
- EMBROIDERY SCISSORS
- 5" × 7" (13 CM × 18 CM) OVAL EMBROIDERY HOOP
- SILK PINS (STRAIGHT PINS WITH GLASS OR METAL HEADS)
- RULER
- #2 PENCIL
- TRACING PAPER
- BLACK FINE-LINE FELT-TIP PEN
- POUNCE POWDER (OR CHALK POWDER)
- COTTONBALLS
- FINE-LINE WATER-SOLUBLE MARKING PEN
- PADDED IRONING BOARD

STITCHES USED
STEM STITCH (PAGE 15)
PADDED SATIN STITCH (PAGE 18)
OVERCAST STITCH (PAGE 18)

SKILL LEVEL
ADVANCED

 ESTIMATED TIME REQUIRED
7–8 HOURS

■ RASPBERRY DMC #8685

Monogrammed Blanket

Add warmth and elegance to your bedroom with a beautiful personalized blanket. Striking raspberry-colored plumes flank the bold monogram, all on a ground of ivory merino wool. Three easy stitches are used to create this sumptuous design: stem stitch, overcast stitch, and padded satin stitch. As always, the color scheme can be modified to suit the décor of your home.

Monogrammed Blanket

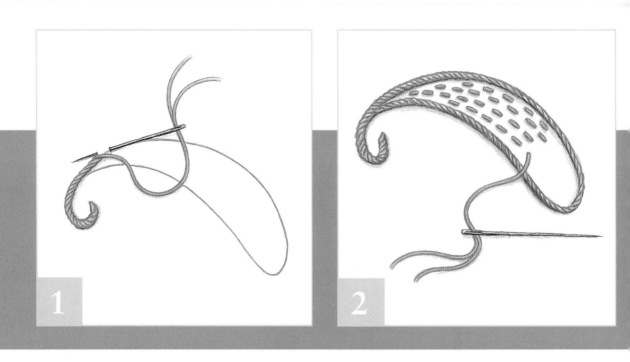

STEP 1   Locate the middle of the blanket's top edge, measure in 7" (18 cm) and mark with a pin. Follow the Pricking and Pouncing instructions (page 13) to transfer the open scroll design (page 116) to the blanket, at the pin marking. In addition, mark two closed scrolls evenly spaced on either side. Thread a #24 chenille needle with two strands of raspberry broder medicis wool. Working from left to right, outline each shape in stem stitch. To stitch the curved plumes, begin at the curled tail and work up the outside curve and around. Stitch each teardrop plume starting and ending at the pointed tip.

STEP 2   Thread a #24 chenille needle with two strands of raspberry broder medicis wool. Beginning at the pointed end of each plume, fill the interior with tiny, randomly spaced straight stitches not exceeding 1/8" (3 mm) in length. Tie off. This technique, called "seeding," provides a padding for the satin stitching that will follow. Seeding stitches are always worked perpendicular to the satin stitches that will cover them.

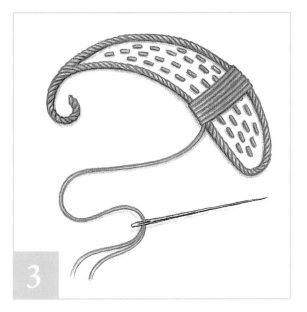

STEP 3 For the satin stitch, thread a #24 chenille needle with two strands of raspberry broder medicis wool. Starting in the middle of each plume, bring the needle and thread to the front of the fabric on the inside curve. Insert the needle into the fabric on the outside curve, and pull the thread through to the back to complete the first stitch. Continue working satin stitch over the seeding to cover the broader end of the plume. Start at the middle and work in the other direction to cover the narrower end.

STEP 4 To add a monogram, draft a 2 $^1/2$" (6 cm) line on tracing paper. Place the paper on monogram alphabet (page 125), center the line horizontally on the desired letter, and trace. Follow the Pricking and Pouncing instructions (page 13) to transfer the monogram to the blanket, centering it between the two embroidered open scrolls. Thread a #24 chenille needle with two strands of raspberry broder medicis wool. Embroider the monogram in overcast stitch.

Use the template patterns on page 116 and the monogram alphabet on page 125.

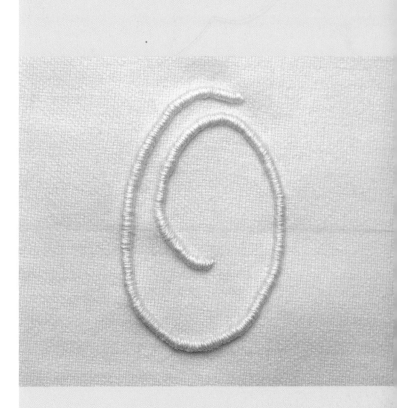

VARIATION

For an understated look, stitch the entire design in ivory-colored yarn. The white-on-white palette will focus attention on the embroidery's texture.

Cherry Blossoms
Lamp Shade

Embroider our delicate pink cherry blossoms on a ground of ivory silk dupioni

and experience for yourself the calming effects of Asian-influenced design.

This classic motif requires four stitches: stem stitch, buttonhole stitch, detached

chain stitch and French knot. Work the embroidery for one of the self-adhesive

lamp shades that are readily available in today's marketplace. If you have

previous experience or expertise in lamp shade crafting, you might adapt the

needlework to one of your own shade designs.

- SELF-ADHESIVE LAMP SHADE
- IVORY SILK DUPIONI FABRIC
  (TO COVER LAMP SHADE)
- IVORY-COLORED TRIM
  (FOR BOTTOM EDGE OF LAMP SHADE)
- IVORY-COLORED FLEXIBLE BINDING
- SIX-STRAND COTTON EMBROIDERY FLOSS;
  WE USED ONE SKEIN EACH OF DMC #3863,
  #818, #3326
- #8 CREWEL NEEDLES
- #9 CREWEL NEEDLES
- EMBROIDERY SCISSORS
- 5" (13 CM) ROUND EMBROIDERY HOOP
- TAPE MEASURE
- SILK PINS (STRAIGHT PINS WITH GLASS
  OR METAL HEADS)
- DRESSMAKER'S CARBON PAPER
- STYLUS
- IRON AND IRONING BOARD

STITCHES USED
STEM STITCH (PAGE 15)
BUTTONHOLE STITCH (PAGE 20)
DETACHED CHAIN STITCH
   (A.K.A. LAZY DAISY) (PAGE 19)
FRENCH KNOT (PAGE 20)

SKILL LEVEL
INTERMEDIATE

ESTIMATED TIME REQUIRED
2–3 HOURS

  COCOA DMC #3863

  COTTON CANDY DMC #818

 ROSE BLUSH DMC #3326

Cherry Blossoms Lamp Shade

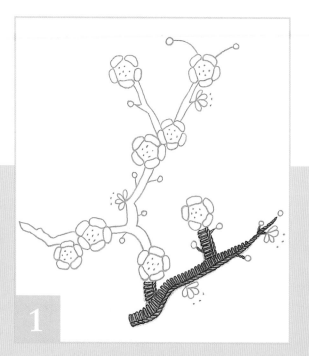

1

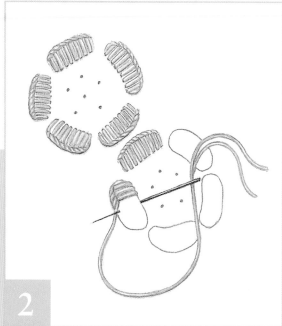

2

STEP 1   Iron the silk to remove any wrinkles. Mark the lamp shade outline on the silk, following the manufacturer's instructions. Mark the cherry blossom design (page 116) on the center front of the lamp shade, using the Dressmaker's Carbon Transfer method (page 12). Thread a #9 crewel needle with two strands of cocoa floss. Embroider the branches in buttonhole stitch. Add the small twigs in stem stitch.

STEP 2   For the cherry blossoms, thread a #9 crewel needle with two strands of cotton candy floss (for a more dramatic look, use two strands of rose blush floss). Work the A blossoms in buttonhole stitch, tying off after each flower. Work the B blossoms the same way, using one strand each of cotton candy and rose blush floss.

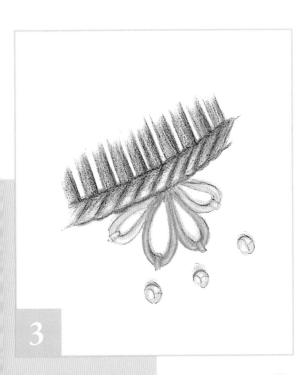

3

STEP 3 For the closed buds, thread a #8 crewel needle with three strands of rose blush floss. Work a 3-wrap French knot for each bud. For the slightly opened buds, thread a #9 crewel needle with two strands of rose blush floss. Work the two inner petals of each bud in detached chain stitch. Change to two strands of cotton candy floss to work the two outside petals. Work the three dots as three one-wrap French knots. Follow the manufacturer's instructions to assemble and trim the lamp shade.

Use the template pattern on page 116.

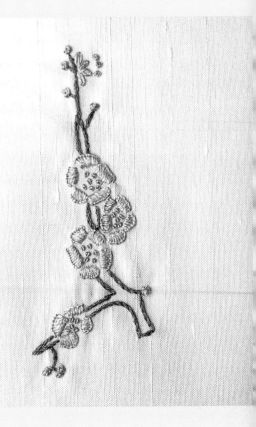

VARIATION

Embroider an abbreviated version of our classic Asian-inspired cherry blossoms around the bottom edge of a small lamp shade. For a lighter look, use stem stitch instead of buttonhole stitch for the branch.

MATERIALS

- WHITE COTTON HEMSTITCHED BED SKIRT
- SIX-STRAND COTTON EMBROIDERY FLOSS; WE USED ONE SKEIN EACH OF DMC #3348, #772, # 3753, #341, AND BLANC
- #9 CREWEL NEEDLES
- #7 BETWEENS NEEDLES
- EMBROIDERY SCISSORS
- 5" × 7" (13 CM × 18 CM) OVAL EMBROIDERY HOOP
- SILK PINS (STRAIGHT PINS WITH GLASS OR METAL HEADS)
- DRESSMAKER'S CARBON PAPER
- STYLUS

STITCHES USED
STEM STITCH (PAGE 15)

DETACHED CHAIN STITCH (A.K.A. LAZY DAISY) (PAGE 19)

FRENCH KNOT (PAGE 20)

SKILL LEVEL
BEGINNER

ESTIMATED TIME REQUIRED
2–3 HOURS

Floral Garlands Bedskirt

What better way to restore your spirit after a hectic day than by spending a quiet moment or two working on your latest embroidery project? Here's a design that will make your bedroom more restful and inviting. Add graceful floral garlands to a hemstitched bedskirt, and you quickly transform your bed into the focal point of the master suite. We selected peaceful shades of blue and green to play against the ground of whisper-soft white cotton—the perfect color scheme for fashioning your own personal retreat. Only three stitches are required: stem stitch, detached chain stitch, and French knot.

SPRING GREEN DMC #3348

SEA GREEN DMC #772

ARCTIC BLUE DMC #3753

CORNFLOWER DMC #341

WHITE DMC BLANC

Floral Garlands Bedskirt

STEP 1 Make two mirror-image copies of the bedskirt template pattern (page 117). Tape both halves together, with the six-petaled flower in the middle. Follow the Dressmaker's Carbon Transfer instructions (page 12) to mark the floral design around the perimeter of the bedskirt, 3" (8 cm) above the hemmed edge. We transferred a total of eight designs: three along each side of the bed and two at the foot of the bed. Thread a #9 crewel needle with one strand each of spring green and leaf green floss. Starting at the left end of each design, embroider the vine and stems in stem stitch. Work the leaves in detached chain stitch. Continue until all of the foliage has been completed.

STEP 2 For the five-petal flowers, thread a #9 crewel needle with one strand each of arctic blue and cornflower floss. Work each petal in detached chain stitch. Work each six-petal flower the same way, except use two strands of cornflower floss.

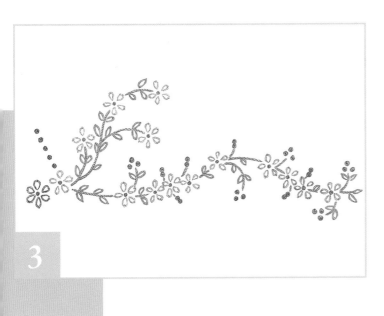

3

Short on time, but still love the look of hand-embroidered bed linens? Then stitch this abbreviated version of our floral garland motif. Using just one color of thread is another way to make the stitching go faster. We chose a vibrant yellow floss so that every day would begin with a little bit of sunshine!

BUTTERCUP DMC #727

STEP 3 For the French knots, thread a #7 betweens needle with two strands of white floss. Work a 2-wrap French knot at the center of every flower. Change to two strands of arctic blue floss. Work the flower sprigs with two buds as two 2-wrap French knots. Work the flower sprigs with three buds as three 3-wrap French knots. Change to two strands of cornflower floss. Work each of the nine dots at the center of the design as a 3-wrap French knot.

Use the template pattern on page 117.

THE EMBROIDERED *Bath*

Shiny brass fixtures that glow by candlelight, smooth ceramic tile that's cool to the touch, an antique claw foot tub filled to the brim with fragrant bubbles—here are the makings of a tranquil refuge where you can relax, pamper yourself, and restore vigor to both body and spirit. Today's bath is more than just a place to take a quick shower; it's a luxuriant retreat that lets you forget life's hassles.

Your own mini-spa will become even more inviting when you add hand-embroidered accessories and bath linens. Whether your taste runs to perky geometric stitchery on a bath towel or classic scroll embroidery on the back of a silver hand mirror, the opportunities for embellishing ordinary as well as specialty bath items are numerous.

Three of the projects in this chapter—fluttery café curtains, soft, plush bath towels, and a sassy shower curtain—are all stitched on ready-made pieces. As with so many of our projects, the appeal of embellishing a purchased item is undeniable. There's no further sewing or assembly, and you can begin using your new piece right away, as soon as the embroidery is finished. If you are more experienced in your stitching, you may want to try our fourth project, an elegant vanity set done in shadow work embroidery. It requires minimal finishing that you can easily do yourself.

There are many ways to adapt our bathroom designs. Different thread colors, different stitches, or even a change of background fabric can give a design a whole new look. Before you try something new, take a look at the project variations for some fresh takes on your spa renovation.

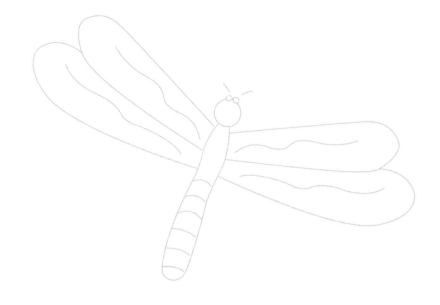

- WHITE COTTON CAFÉ CURTAIN PANELS; OURS MEASURE 42" × 30" (107 CM × 76 CM) EACH
- METALLIC BLENDING FILAMENT; WE USED ONE SPOOL EACH OF KREINIK METALLIC BLENDING FILAMENTS #023 AND #012
- SIX-STRAND COTTON EMBROIDERY FLOSS; WE USED ONE SKEIN EACH OF DMC #208, #209, #702, #703
- #8 CREWEL NEEDLES
- EMBROIDERY SCISSORS
- 5" (13 CM) ROUND EMBROIDERY HOOP
- TAPE MEASURE
- SILK PINS (STRAIGHT PINS WITH GLASS OR METAL HEADS)
- #2 PENCIL
- REMOVABLE TAPE
- SPRAY STARCH
- IRON AND IRONING BOARD

STITCHES USED
STEM STITCH (PAGE 15)
STRAIGHT STITCH (PAGE 16)
FRENCH KNOT (PAGE 20)

SKILL LEVEL
BEGINNER

ESTIMATED TIME REQUIRED
5–6 HOURS FOR EACH PANEL

café curtains

A glittering dragonfly hovers above a lush green meadow, beckoning you to come out and play. Spring will be forever in the air when you add a pair of these gauzy white cotton café curtains to your bath. You'll be amazed at how quick and easy they are to stitch! The design requires three basic stitches: stem stitch, straight stitch, and French knot. As an added bonus, the motif is embroidered on ready-made curtains so there's no finishing involved—just stitch your curtains, hang them in a sunny window, and enjoy!

LILAC METALLIC KREINIK #023

GRAPE METALLIC KREINIK #012

GRAPE DMC #208

LILAC DMC #209

PARROT GREEN DMC #702

GRASSHOPPER DMC #703

café curtains

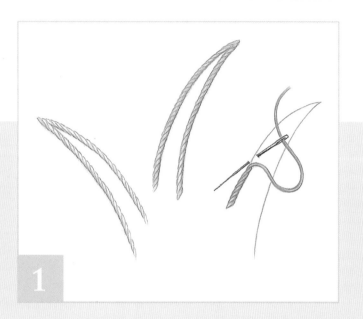

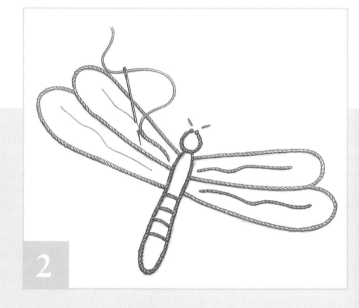

STEP 1 Apply a light coat of spray starch to the entire surface of one curtain panel. Allow two or three minutes for the fabric to absorb the starch, then iron the panel dry. Follow the Direct Tracing Transfer instructions (page 12) to mark one dragonfly/grass design (page 117) on the center of the panel, beginning 10" (25 cm) above the bottom edge. Mark additional grass blades on either side 5" (13 cm) above the bottom edge. Embroider each cluster of three grass blades in stem stitch using a #8 crewel needle. Work each cluster from left to right, using three strands of grasshopper floss for the first blade, one strand of grasshopper and two strands of parrot green for the second blade, and three strands of parrot green for the third blade.

STEP 2 For the dragonfly, thread a #8 crewel needle with two strands of grape floss and one strand of grape blending filament. Work the dragonfly's body and head in stem stitch. Embroider two 3-wrap French knots for the eyes and two 1/8" (3 mm) straight stitches for the antennae. Use one strand of lilac floss and two strands of lilac blending filament to outline the wings in stem stitch. Use one strand each of lilac floss, grape blending filament, and lilac blending filament to work the wing details in stem stitch.

Use the template pattern on page 117.

VARIATION

Substitute a bumblebee for the dragonfly and add a perky tulip to the picture for a quick change of scenery! Use the pattern on page 117. You will need the following additional fibers:

- ■ EBONY DMC #310
- ■ FOG DMC #762
- ■ SUNSHINE YELLOW DMC #726
- ■ GRASSHOPPER DMC #703
- ■ SILVER METALLIC KREINIK #001

Work the tulip in stem stitch: Use two strands of parrot green floss and one strand of grasshopper floss for the stem. Use three strands of lilac floss for the flower. Outline the bumblebee's head and midsection in stem stitch, using three strands of ebony floss. Work ebony straight stitches, about ⅛" (3 mm) long, for the antennae and legs. Outline the remaining two body sections in stem stitch, using three strands of sunshine yellow floss. Outline the wings in stem stitch, using two strands of fog floss and one strand of silver blending filamanent. Work the wing details in straight stitches.

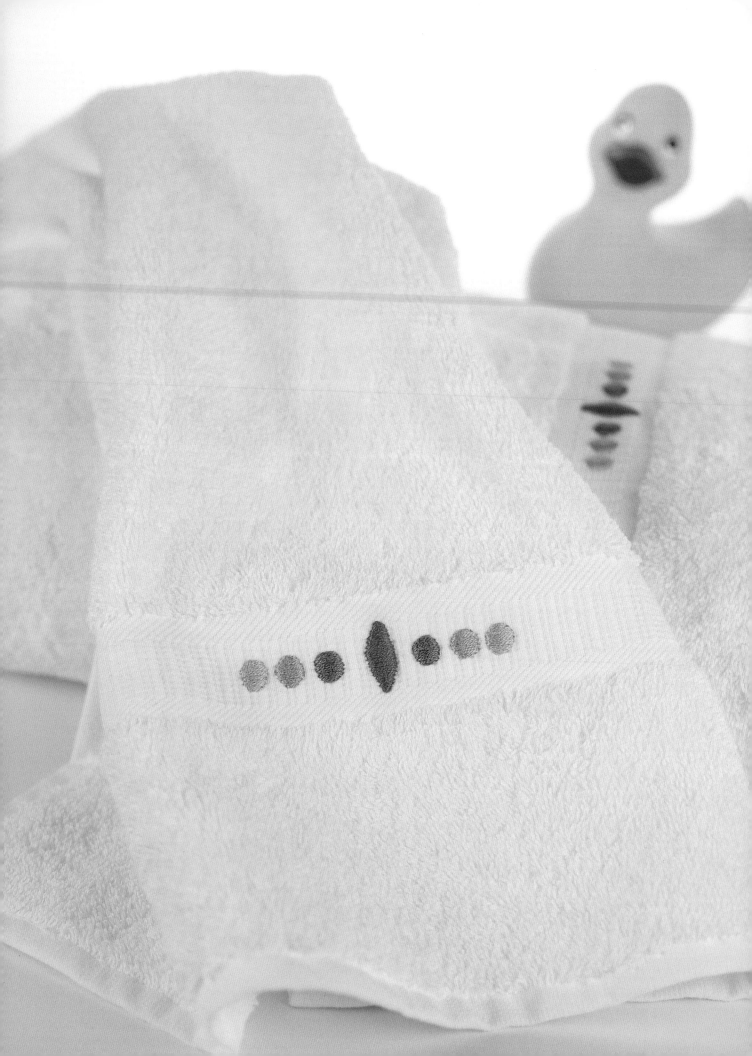

MATERIALS

- WHITE COTTON TERRY CLOTH BATH AND HAND TOWELS
- SIX-STRAND COTTON EMBROIDERY FLOSS; WE USED ONE SKEIN EACH OF DMC #958, #959, #964, #720
- #8 CREWEL NEEDLES
- #24 CHENILLE NEEDLES
- EMBROIDERY SCISSORS
- 5" × 7" (13 CM × 18 CM) OVAL EMBROIDERY HOOP
- TAPE MEASURE
- SILK PINS (STRAIGHT PINS WITH GLASS OR METAL HEADS)
- DRESSMAKER'S CARBON PAPER
- STYLUS

STITCHES USED
BACKSTITCH (PAGE 15)
SATIN STITCH (PAGE 18)

SKILL LEVEL
INTERMEDIATE

ESTIMATED TIME REQUIRED
3–4 HOURS FOR BATH TOWEL
1–2 HOURS FOR HAND TOWEL

Bath Towels

Simple geometric shapes make a clean, bold statement on a set of pristine white terry towels. We chose colors reminiscent of the seaside, but the design would be equally arresting in other bright hues. Choose three different shades of floss to achieve the unique "fading out" effect. The possibilities are endless—just use your imagination!

MERMAID GREEN DMC #958

SEAFOAM DMC #959

ICY AQUAMARINE DMC #964

SUNSET ORANGE DMC #720

Bath Towels

STEP 1 Follow the Dressmaker's Carbon Transfer instructions (page 12) to mark one design motif on the center of each towel's horizontal band. On the bath towel, mark two additional motifs evenly spaced on either side. Thread a #8 crewel needle with two strands of mermaid green floss, and backstitch the two *A* circles of each motif. Backstitch the *B* circles with seafoam floss and the *C* circles with icy aquamarine floss. Backstitch the marquise shape in the middle with sunset orange.

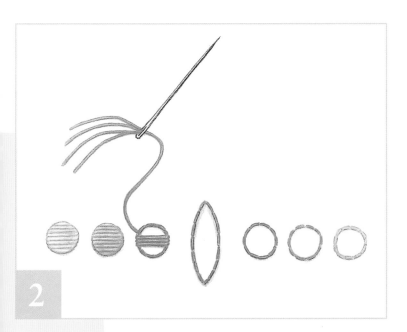

2

STEP 2   Thread a #24 chenille needle with four strands of icy aquamarine floss. Starting at the widest part of the first C circle, bring the needle and thread to the front of the fabric along the edge of the backstitching, insert the needle into the fabric on the opposite side, and pull through to the back to complete the first stitch. Work satin stitches upward to cover the top half of the circle, and end off. Reemerge at the starting point and satin-stitch the lower half of the circle in the same way. Working from left to right, satin-stitch each shape in the design in the appropriate color floss. Remember to use four strands of floss in a #24 chenille needle for good coverage.

Use the template pattern on page 118.

VARIATION

Embroider the same design in colors straight from Provence. Three vivid shades of Mediterranean blue team up with sunshine yellow to add a touch of pastoral France to your bath. Run the satin stitching vertically instead of horizontally for a different stitch texture. Here's the palette:

■ INDIGO DMC #792

■ PERIWINKLE DMC #793

■ MEDITERRANEAN SKY DMC #794

■ SUNSHINE YELLOW DMC #726

MATERIALS

- DENIM SHOWER CURTAIN
- SIX-STRAND COTTON EMBROIDERY FLOSS;
  WE USED THREE SKEINS OF DMC BLANC
  (ALLOW FOR FOUR), ONE SKEIN OF #725.
- #8 CREWEL NEEDLES
- EMBROIDERY SCISSORS
- 4" (10 CM) ROUND EMBROIDERY HOOP
- SILK PINS (STRAIGHT PINS WITH GLASS
  OR METAL HEADS)
- DRESSMAKER'S CARBON PAPER
- STYLUS
- IRON AND IRONING BOARD

STITCHES USED
OVERCAST STITCH (PAGE 18)
BUTTONHOLE STITCH (PAGE 20)

SKILL LEVEL
INTERMEDIATE

ESTIMATED TIME REQUIRED
1 HOUR PER PATTERN REPEAT

Shower Curtain

 WHITE DMC BLANC

 SUNFLOWER DMC #725

Cheerful white flowers float across the top of an indigo denim shower curtain

—the perfect prescription for giving your bath a casual, laid-back ambiance.

The easy floral embroidery is done in overcast stitch and buttonhole stitch.

While we used a ready-made shower curtain, the experienced seamstress may

prefer to buy fabric yardage and sew a curtain using a commercial pattern.

Shower Curtain

STEP 1   Iron the shower curtain to remove any wrinkles. Follow the Dressmaker's Carbon Transfer instructions (page 12) to mark single flowers in between the ring holes across the top of the curtain, starting about 1 ^{1}/2" (4 cm) from the edge. Thread a #8 crewel needle with two strands of sunflower floss. Embroider the swirl at the center of each flower in overcast stitch.

2

STEP 2 Thread a #8 crewel needle with three strands of white floss. Embroider each flower petal in buttonhole stitch. Tie off after each petal.

Use the template pattern on page 118.

VARIATION

The flower design takes on a new look when embroidered in a different color palette. Choose your colors according to the shower curtain background. Against a crisp white cotton shower curtain, peacock blue flowers with vibrant sunshine yellow centers look absolutely stunning. Here's the palette:

 PEACOCK BLUE DMC #312

SUNSHINE YELLOW DMC #726

MATERIALS

- SILVER VANITY SET
- TWO 9" × 9" (23 CM × 23 CM) SQUARES OF WHITE LINEN FABRIC
- SIX-STRAND COTTON EMBROIDERY FLOSS; WE USED ONE SKEIN OF DMC #800
- #9 CREWEL NEEDLES
- #8 CREWEL NEEDLES
- EMBROIDERY SCISSORS
- 5" × 7" (13 CM × 18 CM) OVAL EMBROIDERY HOOP
- SILK PINS (STRAIGHT PINS WITH GLASS OR METAL HEADS)
- DRESSMAKER'S CARBON PAPER
- STYLUS
- SPRAY STARCH
- IRON AND IRONING BOARD

STITCH USED
DOUBLE BACKSTITCH (PAGE 16)

 SKILL LEVEL
ADVANCED

 ESTIMATED TIME REQUIRED
4–5 HOURS FOR THE HAND MIRROR
3–4 HOURS FOR THE HAIRBRUSH

 PASTEL BLUE DMC #800

Vanity Set

Any lady would be delighted to add a magnificent vanity set to her dressing table. This design marries lavish scrolls and swirls with classically simple circle and diamond motifs. All are embroidered in delicate pastel blue on a white linen ground. The finished embroideries are mounted in a silver brush and mirror set for a truly timeless heirloom. Double backstitch is the only stitch used in this project, making it a concentrated study in shadow work embroidery.

vanity set

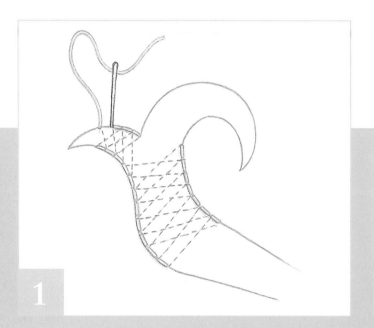

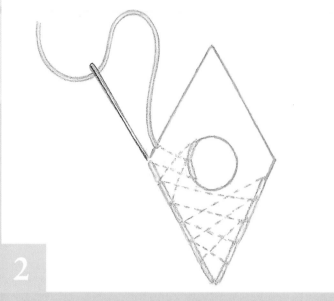

STEP 1   Apply a light coat of spray starch to one square of linen fabric. Allow two or three minutes for the fabric to absorb the starch, then iron the fabric dry. Follow the Direct Tracing Transfer instructions (page 12) to mark the mirror or brush scroll design (page 118) on the fabric. Thread a #9 crewel needle with two strands of pastel blue floss. Begin the shadow work (double backstitch) embroidery on the scroll part of the design, starting at any outside point. Work up the left arm of the V until you reach the place where the design forks into two arches. Stitch the left arch first, remembering to make the stitches on the inside curve slightly smaller/shorter than those on the outside curve. Work the right arch the same way. Weave in the ends on the underside to "shadow" the small open triangle that occurs at the fork. Continue until all the scroll-work is embroidered.

STEP 2   For the diamonds, thread a #9 crewel needle with two strands of pastel blue floss. Begin the double backstitch at the bottom point of the diamond. When you reach the circle, work up toward the left, around the circle, ending at the top of the circle. Weave the needle through the crisscrossed threads on the underside, and reemerge at right side edge where the stitching left off. Work up the right side in the same way and then work both sides to the top point.

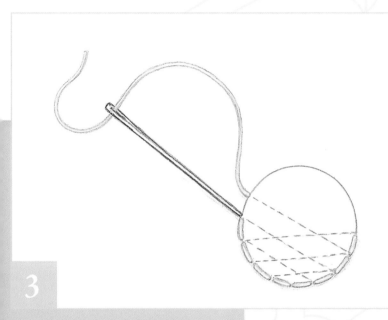

3

STEP 3   For the circles, thread a #8 crewel needle with two strands of pastel blue floss. Make one or more backstitches at the bottom edge of the circle. When the stitches begin to arc upward, begin the side-to-side motion of the double backstitch. Finish off the circle as you started, by making a few backstitches.

Use the template patterns on page 118.

VARIATION

A classic vanity set that can be passed down to future generations is truly a keepsake treasure. Other "icy" pastels, such as pale pink or lavender, would also look elegant against the silverplating. White-on-white is another palette option that never falls out of style, and ecru-on-white looks stunning too!

Sachet Pouch

Perfect for your best friend's birthday, for Mom on Mother's Day, or as a bride's keepsake gift to her wedding attendants, this simple pouch is easy to whip up in advance of special occasions.

Begin with two 5" × 10" (13 cm × 25 cm) strips of pink linen fabric. Fold each strip in half, right side out, so it is square, and finger-press the fold. Unfold one strip and mark the design (page 119) on one square only, using the Direct Tracing Transfer method (page 12). Mount the marked strip in a scroll frame. Embroider each corner scroll design in stem stitch, using two strands of sand floss in a #9 crewel needle.

To construct the pouch, refold both strips, right side out, and press to set the creases. Pin the squares together, embroidery on the inside and raw edges matching. Machine-stitch 1/2" (1 cm) from the raw edges around three sides. Trim the seam allowance to 1/4" (5 mm), clip the corners, and zigzag the raw edges. Turn right side out. Hand-sew ribbon ties to the folded edges in pairs. Tuck potpourri inside the pouch, and tie the ribbons closed.

STITCH USED
STEM STITCH (PAGE 15)

 SAND DMC #644

Picture Frame

STITCH USED
BACKSTITCH (PAGE 15)

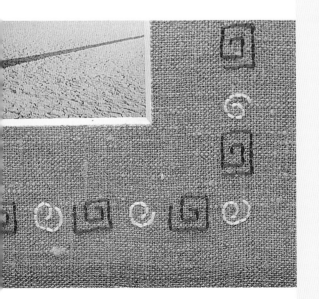

ULTRAMARINE BLUE DMC #825

SNOW WHITE DMC #5200

Whimsical spirals create an eye-catching border around a favorite photograph. Choose thread colors that coordinate with your photo, as we did for this outdoor scene. With motifs this simple, even beginners can create spectacular results.

Start with a 12" × 12" (30 cm × 30 cm) square of raw linen fabric. Transfer the design (page 119) using the Dressmaker's Carbon Transfer method (page 12). Mount the fabric in an oval embroidery hoop. Backstitch the box-shaped spirals first, using two strands of ultramarine blue floss in a #9 crewel needle. Continue all the way around. Then backstitch the circular spirals using two strands of snow white floss.

A professional framer finished our picture frame, but if you have some framing experience, you may wish to complete this step yourself. Purchase an appropriately sized frame and mat for your standard-sized photo. Mount the embroidered fabric on the mat with spray adhesive, making sure it is perfectly centered. Use a sharp mat knife on a protected surface to trim away the excess fabric from the mat opening and around the edges. Mount your photo and the mat in the frame.

Hall Mirror

STITCH USED
STEM STITCH (PAGE 15)

 FOREST GLADE DMC #3052

 WOODLAND MEADOW DMC #3051

Transform an ordinary mirror into a needlework showcase. This handsome project is worked entirely in stem stitch. Subtle shades of green and an elegant satin ribbon hanger complement the walnut frame.

Stiffen a 5" × 7" (13 cm × 18 cm) piece of white linen fabric with iron-on spray starch. Transfer the scroll design (page 119) to the linen using the Direct Tracing Transfer method (page 12). Mount the fabric in an oval hoop so that the design is centered inside the frame. Embroider the four upper scroll motifs in stem stitch, using two strands of forest glade floss in a #9 crewel needle. Repeat to embroider the lower half. Use one strand each of forest glade floss and woodland meadow floss to work the motifs in the middle. Mount the finished embroidery in the display area of the mirror frame.

Crystal Vanity Jar

STITCHES USED

STEM STITCH (PAGE 15)
DETACHED CHAIN STITCH
    (A.K.A. LAZY DAISY) (PAGE 20)
FRENCH KNOT (PAGE 20)
BULLION STITCH (PAGE 21)

PASTEL GREEN DMC #955

PASTEL PINK DMC #3713

BABY BLUE DMC #3325

ROSEBUD DMC #761

LEMON DROP DMC #3078

The beauty of the garden is captured in this circle of delicate flowers designed especially for the lid of a hand-cut lead crystal jar.

Stiffen a 6" × 6" (15 cm × 15 cm) square of white linen fabric with iron-on spray starch. Transfer the floral design (page 120) to the linen using the Direct Tracing Transfer method (page 12). Mount the fabric in a round hoop so that the design is centered inside the frame. Embroider the foliage first, using two strands of pastel green floss in a #9 crewel needle. Work the stems in stem stitch and the leaves in detached chain stitch. Change to two strands of pastel pink. Embroider the daisies in detached chain stitch, tying off after each group of three, or after each single daisy, as appropriate. Thread a #7 betweens needle with two strands of baby blue floss. For each forget-me-not, embroider four 2-wrap French knots as the petals. Tie off after each flower. Thread a #8 milliner's needle with two strands of rosebud floss. Work two 8-wrap bullion stitches side by side to create each bullion rosebud. Tie off after each cluster. For each rose, first work two 5-wrap bullion stitches side by side for the rose center. Change to one strand each of pastel pink and rose-bud floss. Embroider three 9-wrap bullion stitches around each rose center, followed by six 10-wrap bullion stitches. Tie off after completing each rose. Thread a #7 betweens needle with two strands of lemon drop floss. Embroider a 2-wrap French knot at the center of each lazy daisy and forget-me-not. Additional leaves may be added in detached chain stitch if desired.

Trinket Box

Work these cheerful flowers in the tantalizing colors of a tropical sunset—you'll feel like you're in an embroiderer's paradise.

Stiffen a 7" × 9" (18 cm × 23 cm) piece of white linen fabric using iron-on spray starch. Transfer the design (page 120) to the linen using the Direct Tracing Transfer method (page 12). Using two strands of orange blaze floss in a #9 crewel needle, embroider the left daisy's petals in chain stitch. In the same way, embroider the middle daisy with lemon sunshine floss, and the right daisy with turquoise floss. Chain-stitch the center of the middle daisy in orange blaze floss and the centers of the other two daisies in lemon sunshine floss. Tie off after each color change. Work the zigzag borders in interlaced backstitch. Backstitch the outer zigzag lines with two strands of turquoise floss and the inner zigzags with two strands of orange blaze floss. Use a #26 tapestry needle to weave two strands of lemon sunshine floss in and out of the backstitching.

STITCHES USED
CHAIN STITCH (PAGE 19)
INTERLACED BACKSTITCH (PAGE 16)

TURQUOISE DMC #806

ORANGE BLAZE DMC #947

LEMON SUNSHINE DMC #973

Trivet

STITCHES USED
STEM STITCH (PAGE 15)
STRAIGHT STITCH (PAGE 16)

VALENCIA DMC #741

CITRON DMC #742

DARK OLIVE DMC #3011

OLIVE DMC #3012

A lovely citrus design, embroidered on a ready-made linen trivet, protects your dining table with style. This project is perfect for the embroiderer who needs a quick gift or for any stitcher who craves instant gratification. In fact, you can whip up an entire set in a weekend!

Remove the padding from inside the trivet. Press the linen cover with a warm iron to remove any wrinkles. Transfer the citrus design (page 121) to the linen cover using the Dressmaker's Carbon Transfer method (page 12). Mount the fabric in a 3 " (8 cm) round hoop so that the design is centered inside the frame. (Make sure that the inner ring is inside the trivet pocket and that only the top layer of fabric is framed up.) Thread a #9 crewel needle with one strand each of Valencia and citron floss. Working from left to right, outline each orange in stem stitch, and tie off. Change to two strands of Valencia floss. Work the curved lines on each orange in stem stitch and the tiny angular details in straight stitch. Change to one strand each of dark olive and olive floss. Beginning at the lower left, embroider the outline and center vein of each leaf in stem stitch. Tie off after each leaf (or leaf pair) rather than carrying the thread across the back. Reinsert the padding before using the trivet.

Guest Towel

Stitch an enchanting floral spray in splashy shades of azalea, lemon drop, cherry red, orange blaze, and key lime for a stunning twist on an old classic. That's right, this timeless embroidery design takes on a whole new look when worked in snazzy brights.

Begin by stiffening a ready-made white linen guest towel with iron-on spray starch. Use the Direct Tracing Transfer method (page 12) to transfer the design (page 121), centering it on the towel about 5" (13 cm) above the lower edge. Thread a #9 crewel needle with two strands of key lime floss. Embroider the five stems in stem stitch and the leaves in detached chain stitch. Change to two strands of orange blaze floss. Work the daisy petals in detached chain stitch, tying off after each flower. Thread a #7 betweens needle with two strands of cherry red floss. Embroider each posey petal with a 2-wrap French knot, tying off after each flower. Thread a #8 milliners needle with two strands of azalea floss. Work two 8-wrap bullion stitches side by side four times to create the rosebuds in the center of the design. Thread a #9 crewel needle with two strands of key lime floss, and make two lazy daisy leaves at the base of each rosebud. Thread a #7 betweens needle with two strands of lemon drop floss, and work a 2-wrap French knot at the center of each daisy and small red posey. Machine-stitch a length of cherry red rickrack to the towel 1" (3 cm) above the lower edge.

STITCHES USED
STEM STITCH (PAGE 15)
DETACHED CHAIN STITCH
   (A.K.A. LAZY DAISY) (PAGE 19)
FRENCH KNOT (PAGE 20)
BULLION STITCH (PAGE 21)

KEY LIME DMC #906

ORANGE BLAZE DMC #947

CHERRY RED DMC #321

AZALEA DMC #3804

LEMON DROP DMC #3078

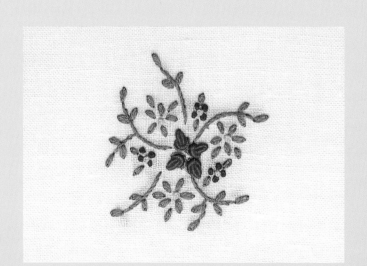

cocktail Napkins

STITCH USED
OVERCAST STITCH (PAGE 18)

 SAND DMC #644

Chic cocktail napkins are classically simple, and they're a breeze to embroider, too! One stitch, one thread color, purchased hemstitched linen squares—what could be easier?

Stiffen a white linen cocktail napkin with iron-on spray starch. Transfer the scroll design (page 121) to one corner of the napkin fabric using the Direct Tracing Transfer method (page 12). To mount the napkin in a hoop so the design is centered, follow the tip for making a false muslin edge (page 14). Thread a #9 crewel needle with two strands of sand floss. Working from left to right, embroider the scrolls in overcast stitch, and tie off. Remove the muslin from the corner of the napkin and discard it. Repeat to embroider each napkin in the set.

Memory Album

Safeguard your precious photos and memorabilia in a monogrammed album—there's just no better way to commemorate life's milestones. Better yet, start a tradition by making an album for each of life's celebrations—births, graduations, weddings, anniversaries.

Choose a commercial pattern and raw linen fabric for your album cover. Cut out the fabric as the pattern directs, and then transfer the heart design (page 122) to the front cover area using the Dressmaker's Carbon Transfer method (page 12). Thread #9 crewel needle with two strands of lilac floss. Mount the fabric on a scroll frame. Beginning at the bottom, work up the left side of the heart shape in chain stitch. Then work up the right side. To add a monogram, use the alphabet on page 125. Draft a 2 $1/2$" (6 cm) line on tracing paper, center the line horizontally on the desired letter, and trace. Use dressmaker's carbon to transfer the monogram to the linen within the embroidered heart. Embroider the monogram in chain stitch, too. Follow the pattern instructions to complete the album cover.

STITCH USED
CHAIN STITCH (PAGE 19)

LILAC DMC #209

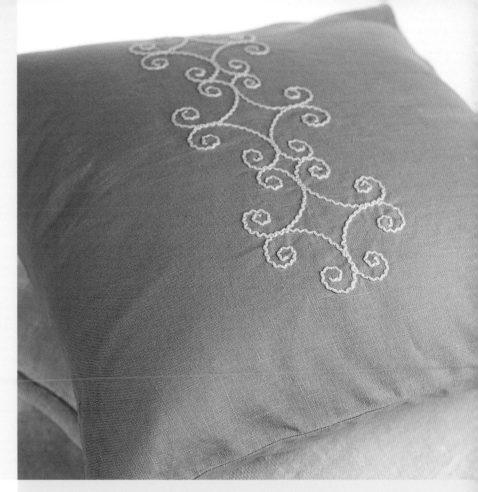

Square Sofa Pillow

STITCH USED

INTERLACED BACKSTITCH (PAGE 16)

WHITE SILK & IVORY YARN #02

To create a one-of-a-kind accessory for your sofa, embellish a purchased linen pillow cover with decorative stitching. This entire design is worked in interlaced backstitch, a combination stitch that is usually worked in two colors. Here, a soft white yarn is used for both parts of the stitch, placing the accent on texture instead.

Unbutton the cover, and remove the pillow insert. Using the Dressmaker's Carbon Transfer method (page 12), mark the scroll design (page 122) three times down the middle of the pillow cover (mark the center design first). Thread a #24 chenille needle with one strand of white yarn. Mount the pillow cover in a 6" (15 cm) round embroidery hoop so the top motif is showing. Starting in the lower left quadrant and working clockwise, embroider each scroll line with 1/8" (3 mm) backstitches, and tie off. Work the two remaining design repeats in the same manner. Use a #28 tapestry needle to weave one strand of white yarn in and out of the backstitches. Press the cover with a warm iron before reinserting the pillow form.

Ladybug Place Mat

This little ladybug, embroidered on a place mat, looks like she's just wandered in from the garden. For an amusing twist, change her location on each place mat you embroider.

Mark the design (page 122) using the Dressmaker's Carbon Transfer method (page 12). Thread a #24 chenille needle with three strands of cherry red floss. Work the ladybug's entire body in satin stitch, and tie off. Change to three strands of ebony floss. Satin-stitch the seven spots on the ladybug's body (see the template diagram), and tie off. Work her head in satin stitch, too. Thread a #8 crewel needle with two strands of ebony floss. Using tiny straight stitches, work the antennae and legs.

STITCHES USED
STRAIGHT STITCH (PAGE 16)
SATIN STITCH (PAGE 18)

 CHERRY RED DMC #321

EBONY DMC #310

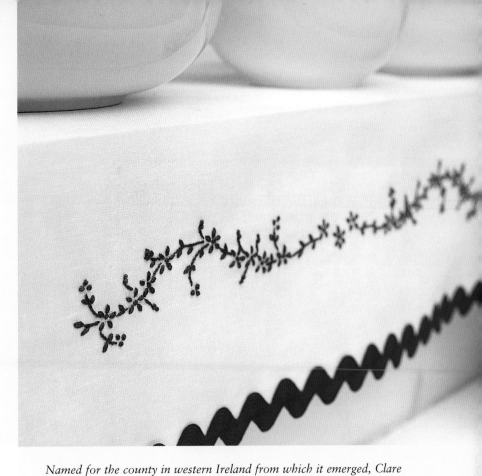

Shelf Cloth

STITCHES USED

STEM STITCH (PAGE 15)

DETACHED CHAIN STITCH
(A.K.A. LAZY DAISY) (PAGE 19)

FRENCH KNOT (PAGE 20)

 COBALT BLUE DMC #797

Named for the county in western Ireland from which it emerged, Clare embroidery is a unique style that dates back to the late nineteenth century. It is traditionally worked on sturdy cotton poplin fabric and has been used to adorn everything from children's clothing to household linens. Make our crisp shelf cloth to add a charming touch o' the Emerald Isle to your home!

You'll need a strip of white cotton fabric, 10" (25 cm) wide and cut 5" (13 cm) shorter than the shelf length. Machine-sew a shirttail hem on all four edges. Stiffen the fabric using iron-on spray starch. Make two mirror-image copies of the floral template pattern (page 123). Tape both halves together, making sure the six-petaled flower is in the middle. Following the Direct Tracing Transfer instructions (page 12), mark the design on the middle of the strip, 3" (8 cm) above the long lower edge. Work the entire design using two strands of cobalt blue floss in a #9 crewel needle. Work the vines and stems in stem stitch and the lazy daisy flowers and leaves in detached chain stitch. Use 2-wrap French knots for the flower centers and 3-wrap French knots for the "dot" flowers. Machine-sew cobalt blue rickrack along the lower edge.

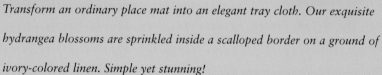

Tray Cloth

Transform an ordinary place mat into an elegant tray cloth. Our exquisite
hydrangea blossoms are sprinkled inside a scalloped border on a ground of
ivory-colored linen. Simple yet stunning!

Use the Direct Tracing Transfer method (page 12) to mark the scalloped
border design (page 123) on the place mat. Work out the full size on tracing
paper first so the scallop falls 1 $^1/_8$" (3 cm) in from the edge all around.
Mark the hydrangea blossoms inside the border in a loose grid arrangement.
Thread a #9 crewel needle with two strands of cornflower floss. Secure a
corner of the place mat in an oval embroidery hoop. Work the scalloped
border in chain stitch all around, moving the hoop as necessary. For the
hydrangeas, change to a 3" (8 cm) round hoop. Using one strand each of
leaf green and spring green floss, work the hydrangea stem in stem stitch
and the leaves in detached chain stitch. For the blossoms, thread a #7
betweens needle with one strand each of cornflower and arctic blue floss.
Embroider a 2-wrap French knot for each blossom to form the flower head.

STITCHES USED

STEM STITCH (PAGE 15)
DETACHED CHAIN STITCH
 (A.K.A. LAZY DAISY) (PAGE 19)
CHAIN STITCH (PAGE 19)
FRENCH KNOT (PAGE 20)

CORNFLOWER DMC #341

SEA GREEN DMC #772

SPRING GREEN DMC #3348

ARCTIC BLUE DMC #3753

Nightgown Case

The old European custom of keeping your nightclothes on top of the bed in a decoratively embroidered case has all but disappeared—until now. Revive an old-fashioned tradition when you make our redwork nightgown case. A contemporary butterfly silhouette updates the classic design.

You'll need 2 yards (1.8 meter) of white cotton fabric, 1 yard (.9 meter) of jumbo rickrack, and sewing notions. Cut off a 1/2-yard piece (1/2-meter) from the fabric, and set the rest aside. Mark the butterfly flap design (page 124) on the 1/2-yard (1/2-meter) piece using the Dressmaker's Carbon Transfer method (page 12). Thread a #9 crewel needle with two strands of cherry red floss. Using an oval hoop, embroider the dots around the edge in padded satin stitch. Tie off after each dot. For the butterfly, use a 6" (15 cm) round hoop. Work the wings and body in padded satin stitch and the antennae in stem stitch. Complete each antenna with a satin stitch dot.

To make the case, cut one front piece, 15 1/2" × 13 7/8" (39 cm × 36 cm), and one back piece, 13 7/8" × 13 7/8" (36 cm × 36 cm), from the reserved fabric. Cut out the embroidered flap on the marked line. Also cut a matching flap lining. Fold under one long edge of the case front, sewing a 2" hem. Sew the front and back together, right sides facing, around three sides. Clip the corners diagonally, turn right side out, and press with a warm iron. Press the straight edge of the flap lining 5/8" (1 cm) to the wrong side. Baste red rickrack to the right side of the embroidered flap along the seam line, clipping at the point if necessary. Sew the flaps right sides together along the basting line, clip as needed, and turn right side out. Sew the flap to the case back, right sides together and raw edges matching. Press the seam allowances to the inside, and slip-stitch the lining closed along the folded edge. Finish by edge-stitching the flap.

STITCHES USED

STEM STITCH (PAGE 15)
PADDED SATIN STITCH (PAGE 18)

CHERRY RED DMC #321

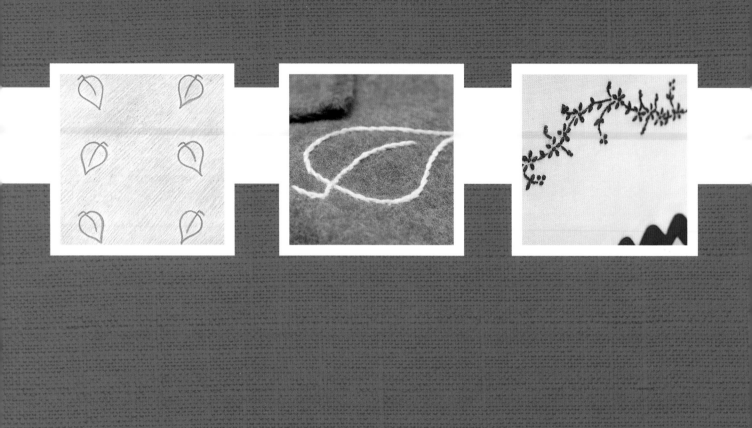

Template Patterns

To work any of the embroidery projects in this book, you will need to use a template pattern. A template is a guide for the stitching that is transferred directly to the embroidery fabric. A description of three different template pattern transfer methods can be found on pages 12-13.

To enlarge a pattern for transferring, use a photocopy machine and set it to the percentage as indicated on the pattern page.

Before transferring the design to fabric, read through the project instructions and study the illustrations to be sure you understand the procedures required to successfully complete the piece. Be sure to match the alignment markings on the patterns (represented by dashed lines) with the straight grain of the fabric before you begin marking. If you have questions or run into difficulty, ask your local needlework shop owner or one of your stitching friends for some help. Refer to the Resource Guide (page 126) for additional assistance.

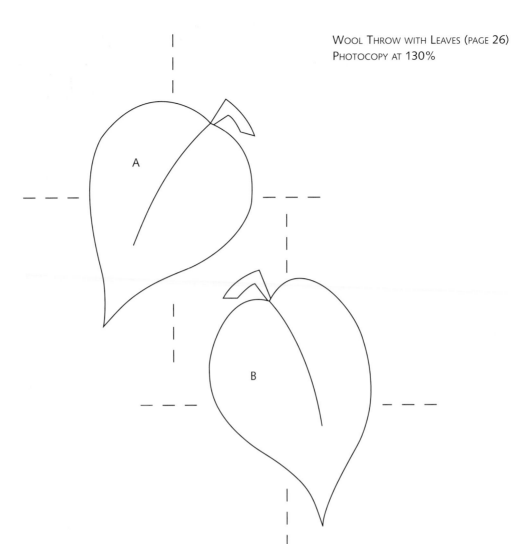

A

B

OVERLAP MIRROR-IMAGE PHOTOCOPY AND TAPE HERE

OVERLAP MIRROR-IMAGE PHOTOCOPY AND TAPE HERE

SILK SOFA PILLOW (PAGE 30)
PHOTOCOPY AT 155%

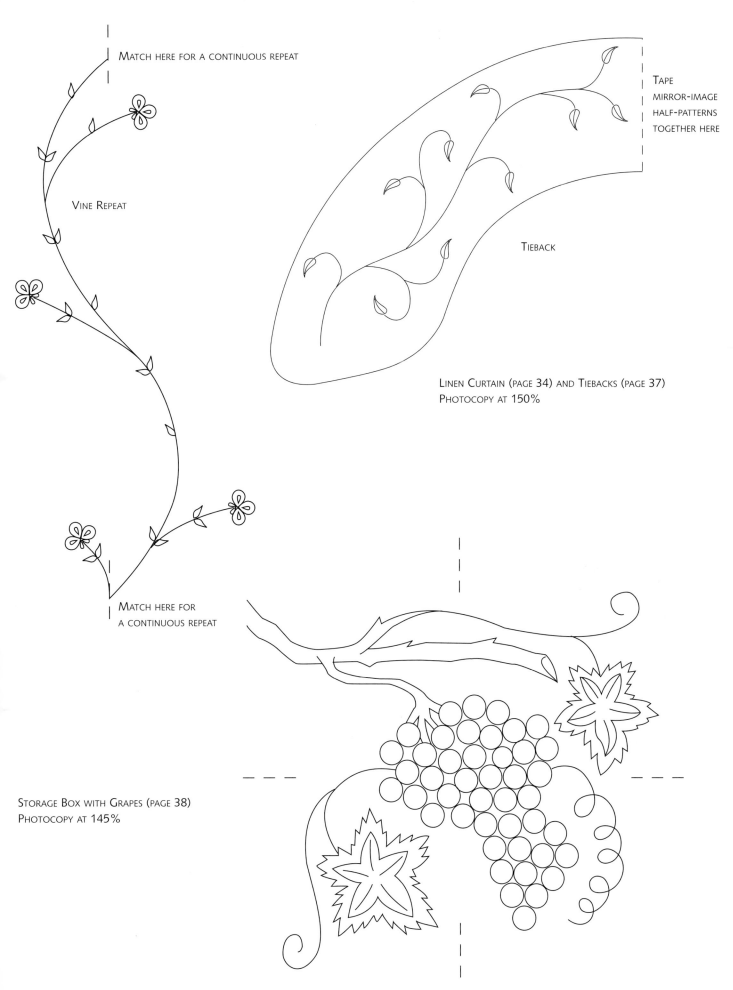

MATCH HERE FOR A CONTINUOUS REPEAT

VINE REPEAT

TAPE
MIRROR-IMAGE
HALF-PATTERNS
TOGETHER HERE

TIEBACK

LINEN CURTAIN (PAGE 34) AND TIEBACKS (PAGE 37)
PHOTOCOPY AT 150%

MATCH HERE FOR
A CONTINUOUS REPEAT

STORAGE BOX WITH GRAPES (PAGE 38)
PHOTOCOPY AT 145%

PANSY TEA COZY (PAGE 44)
PHOTOCOPY AT 130%

TIE-ON CHAIR CUSHION WITH CHERRIES (PAGE 48)
PHOTOCOPY AT 100%

KITCHEN TOWEL WITH APPLE MOTIF (PAGE 52)
PHOTOCOPY AT 100%

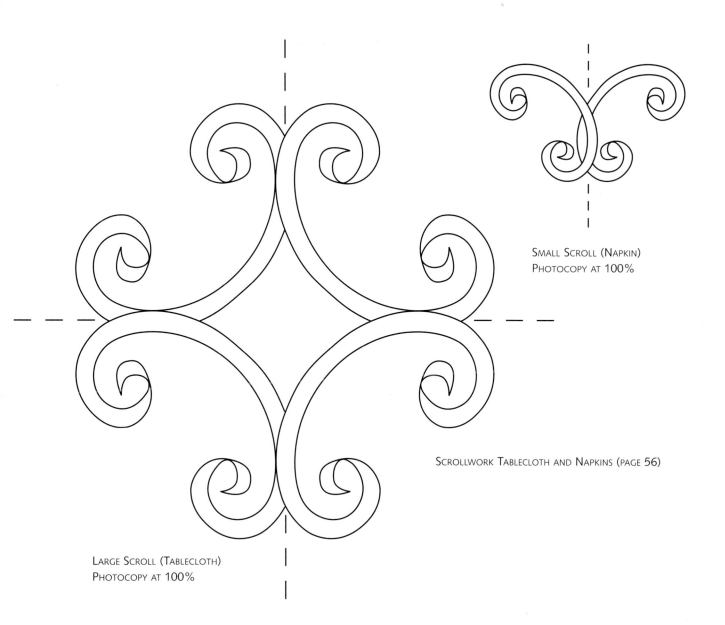

SMALL SCROLL (NAPKIN)
PHOTOCOPY AT 100%

SCROLLWORK TABLECLOTH AND NAPKINS (PAGE 56)

LARGE SCROLL (TABLECLOTH)
PHOTOCOPY AT 100%

BED LINENS (PAGE 62)
PHOTOCOPY AT 100%

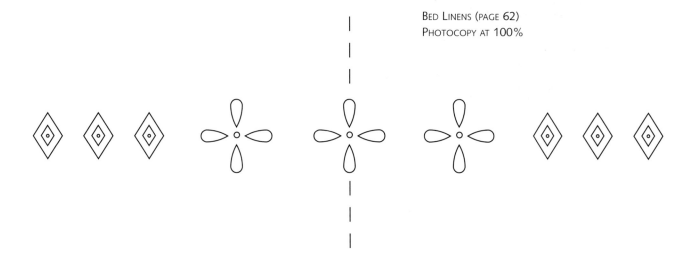

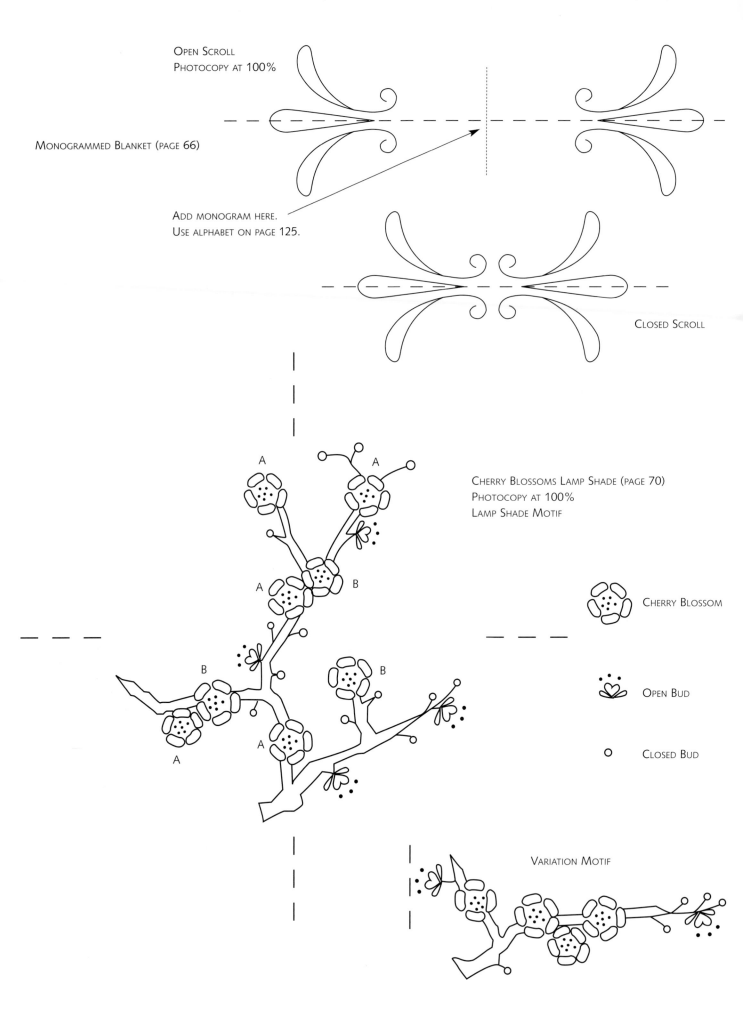

OPEN SCROLL
PHOTOCOPY AT 100%

MONOGRAMMED BLANKET (PAGE 66)

ADD MONOGRAM HERE.
USE ALPHABET ON PAGE 125.

CLOSED SCROLL

A

A

A   B

B

B

A

A

CHERRY BLOSSOMS LAMP SHADE (PAGE 70)
PHOTOCOPY AT 100%
LAMP SHADE MOTIF

CHERRY BLOSSOM

OPEN BUD

CLOSED BUD

VARIATION MOTIF

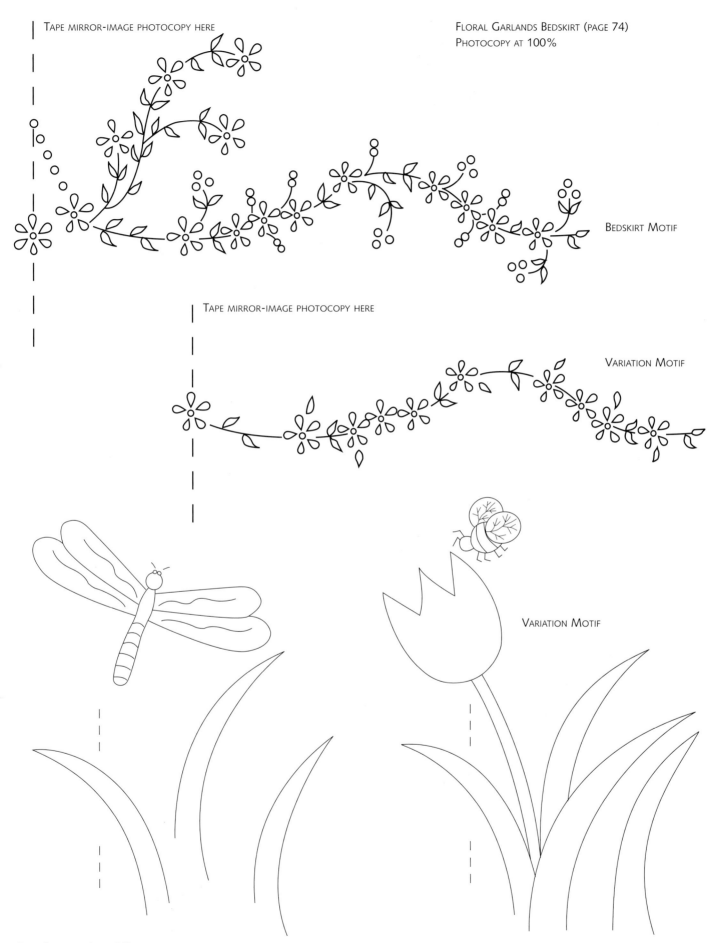

TAPE MIRROR-IMAGE PHOTOCOPY HERE

FLORAL GARLANDS BEDSKIRT (PAGE 74)
PHOTOCOPY AT 100%

BEDSKIRT MOTIF

TAPE MIRROR-IMAGE PHOTOCOPY HERE

VARIATION MOTIF

VARIATION MOTIF

CAFÉ CURTAINS (PAGE 80)
PHOTOCOPY AT 200%

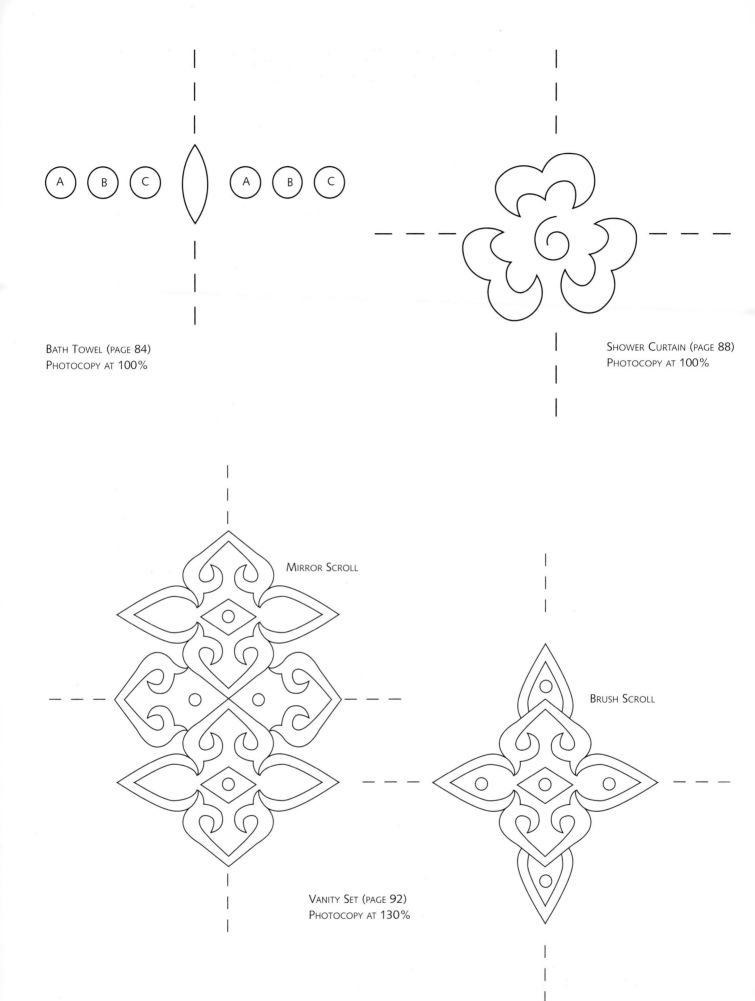

BATH TOWEL (PAGE 84)
PHOTOCOPY AT 100%

SHOWER CURTAIN (PAGE 88)
PHOTOCOPY AT 100%

MIRROR SCROLL

BRUSH SCROLL

VANITY SET (PAGE 92)
PHOTOCOPY AT 130%

FOLD HERE

SACHET POUCH (PAGE 96)
PHOTOCOPY AT 100%

PICTURE FRAME (PAGE 97)
PHOTOCOPY AT 100%

HALL MIRROR (PAGE 100)
PHOTOCOPY AT 130%

CRYSTAL VANITY JAR (PAGE 99)
PHOTOCOPY AT 110%

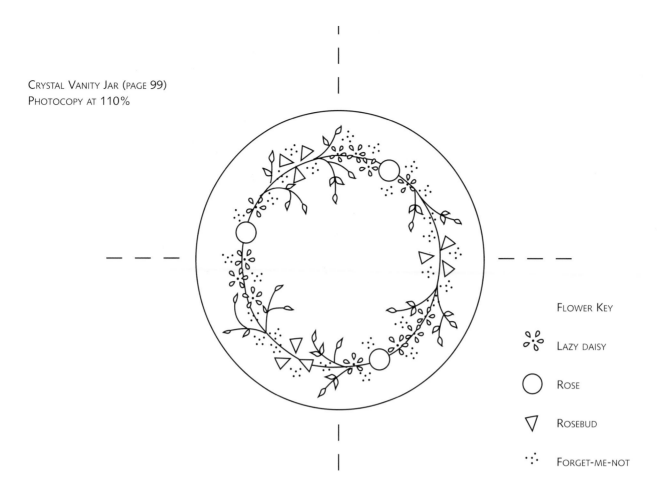

FLOWER KEY

LAZY DAISY

ROSE

ROSEBUD

FORGET-ME-NOT

TRINKET BOX (PAGE 100)
PHOTOCOPY AT 100%

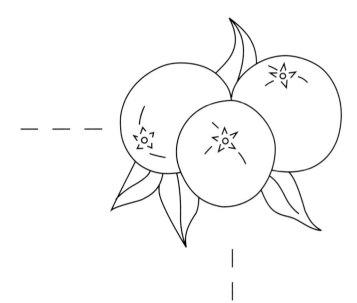

TRIVET (PAGE 101)
PHOTOCOPY AT 100%

GUEST TOWEL (PAGE 102)
PHOTOCOPY AT 100%

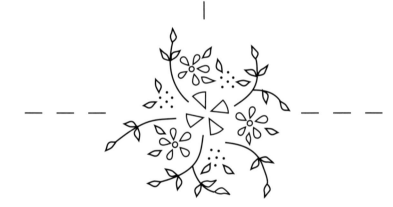

FLOWER KEY

 ROSEBUD

 POSEY

 LAZY DAISY

COCKTAIL NAPKINS (PAGE 103)
PHOTOCOPY AT 100%

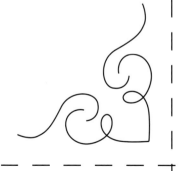

SQUARE SOFA PILLOW (PAGE 105)
PHOTOCOPY AT 140%

X
ADD MONOGRAM HERE.
USE ALPHABET ON PAGE 125.

LADYBUG PLACE MAT (PAGE 106)
PHOTOCOPY AT 100%

MEMORY ALBUM (PAGE 104)
PHOTOCOPY AT 130%

TAPE MIRROR-IMAGE
PHOTOCOPY HERE

SHELF CLOTH (PAGE 107)
PHOTOCOPY AT 100%

TRAY CLOTH (PAGE 108)
PHOTOCOPY AT 130%

NIGHTGOWN CASE (PAGE 109)
PHOTOCOPY AT 145%

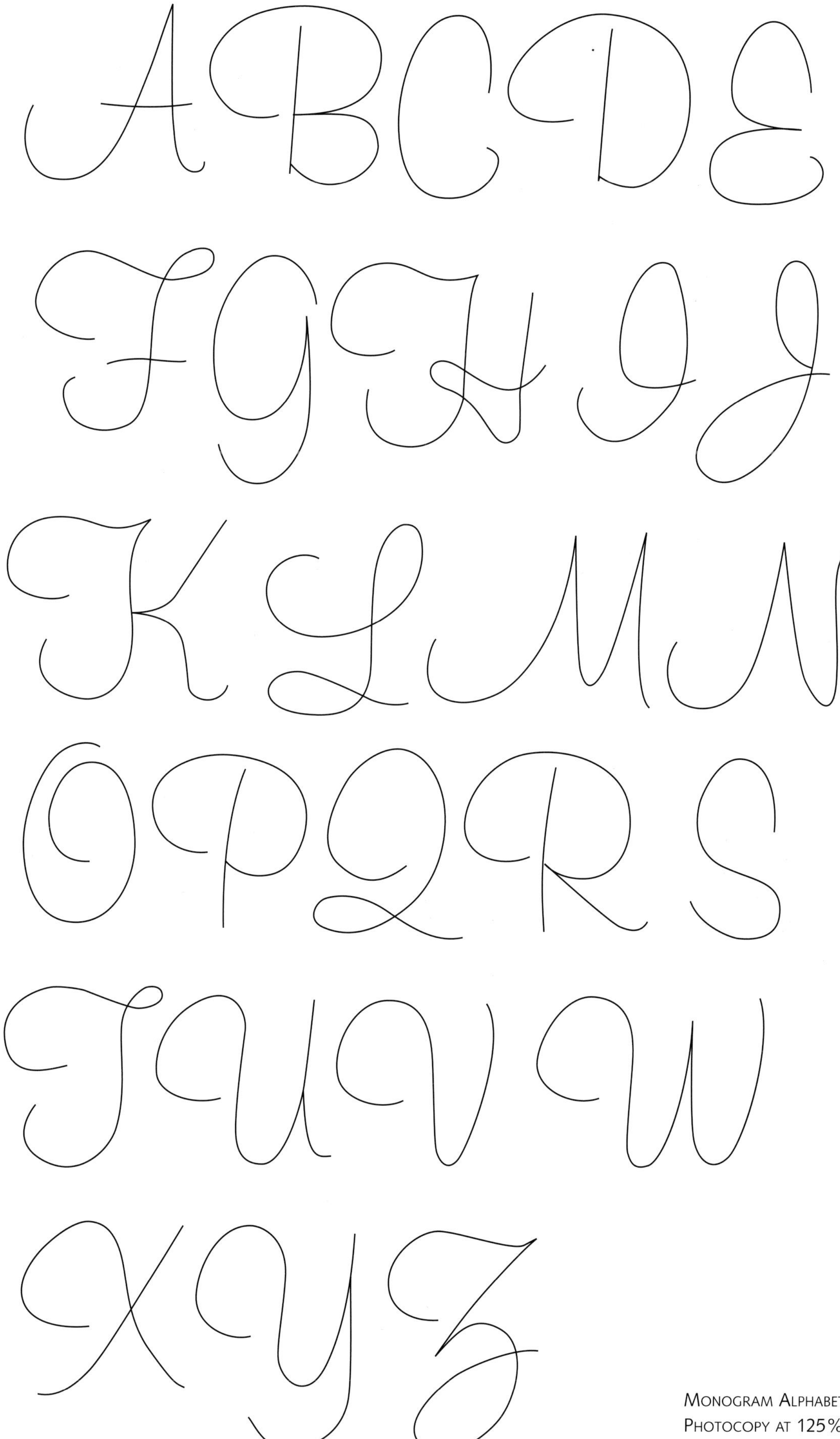

A B C D E

F G H I J

K L M N

O P Q R S

T U V W

X Y Z

MONOGRAM ALPHABET
PHOTOCOPY AT 125%

Resource Guide

Ellen Moore Johnson Designs
3806 Somerset Place
Tuscaloosa, AL 35405-2757
(888) 248-4743
http://www.heirloomembroidery.com
Embroidery patterns, embroidery needles,
instructional video tapes, fine fabrics, and
ready-made linens for embroidery projects

(tea cozy, kitchen towels, tablecloth and
napkins, bed linens, trivet, guest towel
and cocktail napkin; fabrics for storage box,
vanity set, sachet pouch, picture frame,
hall mirror, crystal jar, trinket box,
memory album cover, curtain tieback)

Brown Paper Packages
18 Grand Lake
Ft. Thomas, KY 41075
Fine fibers for needlework

(Merino/silk yarn)

Creative Furnishings
12357 Saraglen Drive
Saratoga, CA 95070
(408) 996-7745
Finely handcrafted wood products designed
especially for display of needlework

(mahogany storage box)

The DMC Corporation
South Hackensack Avenue
Port Kearny Building 10A
South Kearny, NJ
07032-4688
(973) 589-0606
http://www.dmc-usa.com

Fine embroidery fibers

(six-strand cotton embroidery floss
and broder medici)

Garnet Hill
231 Main Street
Franconia, NH 03580
(800) 622-6216
http://www.garnethill.com

High-quality bed linens, pillows, curtains,
furniture, and clothing made of natural
fibers

(Merino wool blanket)

Gay Bowles Sales, Inc.
P. O. Box 1060
Janesville, WI 53547
(800) 356-9438
http://www.millhill.com

Distributor of Framecraft products

(lead crystal jar and vanity set)

Hancock Fabrics
2605A West Main Street
Tupelo, MS 38801
(662) 844-7368
http://www.hancockfabrics.com

Patterns, fabrics, sewing notions

(silk dupioni lamp shade fabric, lamp shade
trim, cotton fabric for nightgown case and
shelf cloth)

Kreinik Manufacturing Co., Inc.
3106 Timanus Lane
Suite 101
Baltimore, MD 21244
(410) 281-0040
http://www.kreinik.com
Fine embroidery fibers
(metallic blending filament)

L. L. Bean
Freeport, ME 04033
(800) 221-4221
http://www.llbean.com
Catalog with a variety of linens
for the home
(wool throw)

Pottery Barn
Mail Order Department
P. O. Box 7044
San Francisco, CA 94120-7044
(800) 922-9934 (call for the store
nearest you.)
http://www.potterybarn.com
Bed, bath, and kitchen linens, also window
treatments and throws

(silk sofa cushion, linen curtain, cotton bed
skirt, cotton bath towels, square sofa pillow,
ladybug place mat)

Sudberry House
12 Colton Road
East Lyme, CT 06333
(800) 243-2607
http://www.sudberry.com
Fine wood accessories for needlework

(hall mirror, trinket box)

The Embroiderers' Guild of America
335 West Broadway
Suite 100
Louisville, KY 40202
(502) 589-6956
http://www.egausa.org
Nonprofit organization dedicated to the
advancement of embroidery

Embroidery Floss Color Conversions

NUMERICAL

DMC	COLOR NAME	ANCHOR
#B5200	snow white	#1
Blanc	white	#2
Ecru	ecru	#387
#208	grape	#110
#209	lilac	#109
#310	ebony	#403
#312	peacock blue	#979
#320	dark leaf green	#215
#321	cherry red	#9046
#341	cornflower	#117
#368	leaf green	#214
#420	chestnut	#374
#434	light brown	#310
#498	dark red	#1005
#550	purple	#102
#552	violet	#99
#554	lavender	#96
#597	aquamarine	#1064
#598	icy aqua	#1062
#644	sand	#830
#702	parrot green	#226
#703	grasshopper	#238
#720	sunset orange	#326
#725	canary yellow	#305
#726	sunshine yellow	#295
#727	buttercup	#293
#741	Valencia	#304
#742	citron	#303
#761	rosebud	#1021
#762	fog	#234
#772	sea green	#259
#792	indigo	#941
#793	periwinkle	#176
#794	Mediterranean sky	#175
#797	cobalt blue	#132
#800	pastel blue	#144
#806	turquoise	#169
#815	crimson	#43
#818	cotton candy	#23
#825	ultramarine blue	#162
#841	taupe	#1082
#869	brown	#944
#905	grass	#257
#906	key lime	#256
#947	orange blaze	#330
#955	pastel green	#206
#958	mermaid green	#187
#959	seafoam	#186
#964	icy aquamarine	#185
#972	sunflower	#298
#973	lemon sunshine	#297
#988	green apple	#243
#3011	dark olive	#846
#3012	olive	#844
#3046	wheat	#887
#3051	woodland meadow	#681
#3052	forest glade	#262
#3078	lemon drop	#292
#3325	baby blue	#129
#3326	rose blush	#36
#3346	lime peel green	#267
#3348	spring green	#264
#3362	jade	#263
#3364	moss	#260
#3713	pastel pink	#1020
#3753	arctic blue	#1031
#3804	azalea	#63
#3863	cocoa	#379

ALPHABETICAL

COLOR NAME	DMC	ANCHOR
aquamarine	#597	#1064
arctic blue	#3753	#1031
azalea	#3804	#63
baby blue	#3325	#129
brown	#869	#944
buttercup	#727	#293
canary yellow	#725	#305
cherry red	#321	#9046
chestnut	#420	#374
citron	#742	#303
cobalt blue	#797	#132
cocoa	#3863	#379
cornflower	#341	#117
cotton candy	#818	#23
crimson	#815	#43
dark leaf green	#320	#215
dark olive	#3011	#846
dark red	#498	#1005
ebony	#310	#403
ecru	ecru	#387
fog	#762	#234
forest glade	#3052	#262
grape	#208	#110
grass	#905	#257
grasshopper	#703	#238
green apple	#988	#243
icy aqua	#598	#1062
icy aquamarine	#964	#185
indigo	#792	#941
jade	#3362	#263
key lime	#906	#256
lavender	#554	#96
leaf green	#368	#214
lemon drop	#3078	#292
lemon sunshine	#973	#297
light brown	#434	#310
lilac	#209	#109
lime peel green	#3346	#267
Mediterranean sky	#794	#175
mermaid green	#958	#187
moss	#3364	#260
olive	#3012	#844
orange blaze	#947	#330
parrot green	#702	#226
pastel blue	#800	#144
pastel green	#955	#206
pastel pink	#3713	#1020
peacock blue	#312	#979
periwinkle	#793	#176
purple	#550	#102
rose blush	#3326	#36
rosebud	#761	#1021
sand	#644	#830
sea green	#772	#259
seafoam	#959	#186
snow white	#B5200	#1
spring green	#3348	#264
sunflower	#972	#298
sunset orange	#720	#326
sunshine yellow	#726	#295
taupe	#841	#1082
turquoise	#806	#169
ultramarine blue	#825	#162
Valencia	#741	#304
violet	#552	#99
wheat	#3046	#887
white	Blanc	#2
woodland meadow	#3051	#681

Acknowledgments

You would not be holding this book in your hands if the wonderful people listed below had not been so gracious in sharing their incredible gifts and talents. I will be forever grateful:

- to Mary Ann Hall for her support of my work from the very beginning. Without her help, I would not have had the opportunity to write this book. Thank you, Mary Ann, for encouraging me to share my love of embroidery with others.

- to Martha Wetherill and Shawna Mullen. Thank you for inviting me to write *The Embroidered Home*.

- to Linda Clark for so graciously allowing me to haunt her beautiful shop, Foxgloves Alley, while selecting fibers for the projects—and for her invaluable advice and encouragement throughout the entire project.

- to Candie Frankel for her painstaking attention to detail when checking (and rechecking) the manuscript, and for her superb organizational skills in pulling all of the pieces together and making them fit.

- to Judy Love for her flawless Stitch Library illustrations and to Lorraine Dey for drawing resplendently impeccable step-by-step illustrations and project diagrams.

- to Susan Raymond for her brilliance in photographic styling and to Bobbie Bush for capturing it on film.

- to Leslie Haimes for taking the text and photographs and so artfully designing such a magnificent book.

- to Manon Kavesky for her visionary creativity in marketing *The Embroidered Home*.

Finally, and most importantly, thank you to my family for putting up with all the disarray so I could complete this project. Your constant encouragement and reassurance, coupled with your unconditional love, mean more than you'll ever know.

About the Author

Ellen Moore Johnson is a designer, writer, and teacher who specializes in plain and fancy needlework, with an emphasis on surface embroidery. She began her adventure in the needle arts at the ripe old age of seven under the tutelage of her grandmothers. (Her first project was a dime store dresser scarf that she proudly embellished with harvest gold embroidery floss!)

A former needlework shop owner, Ellen brings more than fifteen years of teaching experience to her students. Her articles have appeared in numerous publications, and she is an advocate for the preservation and perpetuation of needlework as a fine art through her memberships in a variety of guilds and associations.

Ellen currently lives with her family in Tuscaloosa, Alabama. She considers herself incredibly blessed to have been able to pursue her lifelong hobby as a career.